MERSEYSIDE MARITIME MUSEUM

FRIENDS MAGAZINE

EMERALD

STEPHENSON CLARKE SHIPPING

A brief chronology and history of the ships owned and managed for associated companies

by

Craig J. M. Carter

Published by The World Ship Society
Kendal LA9 7LT
1981

FOREWORD

Stephenson Clarke is one of the oldest, if not the oldest, names in British shipping. Its origins can be traced back to 1730, when the brothers Ralph and Robert Clarke, of North Shields, master mariners, began to buy shares in sailing ships. This book contains a brief chronology of the company's development and a fleet list of the ships owned by Stephenson Clarke and associated companies from 1865 to 1981 — the period in which power-driven ships have flown the company houseflag. Over the years Stephenson Clarke have also managed a large number of ships for public utility undertakings — gas, electricity, water and other authorities, as well as Government-owned ships in wartime. These ships will be the subject of a second book to be published at a later date.   C.J.M.C.

ACKNOWLEDGMENTS

For their help in the preparation of this book, I am indebted to Lloyd's Register of Shipping (Shipping Information Services), Lloyd's Collection at the Guildhall Library, London, members of the staff of Stephenson Clarke Shipping Ltd., L. L. von Munching, Michael Crowdy and members of the World Ship Society Central Record team, and the late Douglas Ridley Chesterton. The cover was designed by Tom Adams and photographs have been supplied by the photographers, etc, as credited in the text.

ISBN 0 905617 17 7

STEPHENSON CLARKE
1730-1981

KING GEORGE II had been on the throne of England for just three years when the brothers Ralph and Robert Clarke purchased an interest in a 300-ton sailing vessel. The year was 1730 and their limited trading activities were to develop during the next 250 years into the present shipowning and ship management business of Stephenson Clarke Shipping Ltd.

Sons of Rev. Ralph Clarke, vicar of Long Benton, near North Shields, the two brothers took up seafaring careers, becoming master mariners. They began buying shares in ships, in this way gradually establishing themselves as shipowners, although they also continued to serve at sea for some time.

Robert Clarke had two sons, John and Ralph. The former married Jane Stephenson, of North Shields, in 1775 and moved to London, where he was later joined by his brother to carry on the business of shipowners and coal factors. Thus were laid the foundations of the present shipping organisation, a member of the Powell Duffryn Group since 1928.

1730   Ralph and Robert Clarke bought shares in the sailing vessel Cleveland, engaged in the North American trade.

1775   John Clarke, son of Robert Clarke, married Jane Stephenson, and moved to London, to set up in business with his brother Ralph as shipowners. They also represented their father's and uncle's business in the capital.

1792   John Clarke died, his wife taking his place in the business.

1805   Ralph Clarke took a new partner, J. Burgess, Jane Clarke having retired four years earlier. The firm became known as Clarke & Burgess, setting up offices at 4 St. Dunstan's Alley, near the Coal Exchange. Stephenson Clarke's headquarters remained on approximately the same site until 1973.

1806   John Clarke's eldest son, Robert, joined the firm.

1849   Robert Clarke died at the age of 67. His second son, Stephenson, was already in the business and it fell to him to take over from his father.

1850   Stephenson Clarke & Company was formed.

1865   First recorded steamers, M. E. CLARKE, C. S. BUTLER and J. M. STRACHAN, built by Palmer's, Jarrow, for the company.

1870   Stephenson Clarke signed a contract to carry 15,200 tons of coal to Southampton gas works, varying from 2,400 tons to 800 tons in monthly quantities. For almost the next 100 years the company's ships supplied the Southampton works until carbonisation ceased in 1968.

1872   The steamer SHOREHAM (I) was the first to carry the name of a Sussex town. The company's policy has been, in general, to name its ships after Sussex and Hampshire towns and villages since then.

1888   First steel steamer, the PORTSLADE, (I) built for the fleet by R. Thompson & Sons, Sunderland.

1891   Stephenson Clarke died and was succeeded by his two sons, Col. Stephenson Clarke and Charles B. O. Clarke.

1912   The Gas Light & Coke Company acquired its first steam collier, FULGENS. Stephenson Clarke & Company appointed managers.

1915   First working association with the Powell Duffryn Steam Coal Company, by the formation of the Normandy Shipping Co. Ltd.

1921   The association with Powell Duffryn was strengthened by the formation of Maris Export & Trading Co. Ltd. Partners were Powell Duffryn Steam Coal Company and Stephenson Clarke & Company. Share capital £250,000.

1922	The partnership of Stephenson Clarke & Company was registered as a private limited company, the existing partners, Col. Stephenson Clarke, Charles B. O. Clarke, Sir Stephenson H. Kent, Sir John S. Hindley, Mr. Fred G. Pilley and Mr. Ralph S. Clarke forming the board.
1925	Last ships of the Normandy Shipping Co. Ltd. were sold.
1928	Col. Stephenson Clarke retired. Stephenson Clarke & Co. Ltd. placed in voluntary liquidation and a new company, Stephenson Clarke and Associated Companies Ltd. formed, with Sir Stephenson Kent as chairman. All other directors remained with the new company. In December 1928 Powell Duffryn Steam Coal Co. Ltd. acquired the whole of the ordinary share capital.
1932	Stephenson Clarke & Associated Companies Ltd. were appointed managers of the London Power Company's fleet of colliers.
1933	In a joint venture with William Cory & Son, Ltd. Coal Distributors (South Wales) Ltd. was formed.
1936	Fulham Borough Council appointed the company managers of its new collier fleet, followed at the end of the year by Brighton Corporation, who had taken delivery of two colliers to supply its power station at Shoreham.

BOWCOMBE (I) *G. A. Osbon*

1941	Company headquarters at 4 St. Dunstan's Alley, London EC3 were totally destroyed by enemy action during the night of May 10-11. Temporary offices at 4 Fenchurch Avenue occupied.
1945	Style of Stephenson Clarke & Associated Companies Ltd. was altered to Stephenson Clarke Ltd.
1946	Coastwise Colliers Ltd. formed in March with three other partners to carry out long-term charter for the County of London Electricity Supply Company. BOWCOMBE (I) transferred to the new company and renamed COLWYN.
1947	First motorship for Stephenson Clarke, the SEAFORD (II), built by S. P. Austin & Son Ltd., Sunderland.
1948	Electricity industry nationalised, April 1. The 19 vessels owned by the individual undertakings were vested in the British Electricity Authority but management remained with Stephenson Clarke. Half-share in John Kelly, Ltd., Belfast, acquired.
1949	Gas industry nationalised, May 1. Fleet of the Gas Light & Coke Company vested in the North Thames Gas Board, but management remained with Stephenson Clarke. Coastwise Colliers Ltd. wound up.

4

SEAFORD (II)   *T. Rayner*

1950   First self-propelled hopper barges managed for the British Electricity Authority.
1956   New headquarters building completed on a site partly occupied by the old St. Dunstan's Alley offices, with entrance at 8 Great Tower Street, London EC3, housing the principal offices of Powell Duffryn Ltd. and Stephenson Clarke Ltd. together with a number of subsidiary companies.
1957   First tankers, CHAILEY and STANSTED, built by Grangemouth Dockyard Co. Ltd. and Henry Scarr Ltd., entered service.
1958   Diversification into world-wide trading with the delivery of the motorship CLEVELAND, 12,700 tons deadweight, from William Gray & Co. Ltd., West Hartlepool. Management of first LNG carrier METHANE PIONEER undertaken in association with Conch Methane.

CHAILEY   *G. A. Osbon*

1963   Stephenson Clarke bought the motorship BROUGHTY from Dundee, Perth & London Shipping Co. Ltd. and converted her to LPG carrier ABBAS — second of the name in the fleet.

ABBAS (II)   *Alex Duncan*

1968   Company style changed to Stephenson Clarke Shipping Ltd. reflecting its pre-eminent role as a shipping company.
1970   Powell Duffryn Ltd. acquired William Robertson Shipowners Ltd., Glasgow, with fleet of 10 motorships.
1973   Stephenson Clarke Shipping Ltd. moved headquarters to Europe House, World Trade Centre, London E1, following the disposal by Powell Duffryn Ltd. of the office block at 8 Great Tower Street, EC3. Powell Duffryn headquarters re-located at Stanhope Gate, London.
1975   Two large bulk carriers, DALLINGTON and DONNINGTON, each 12,000 tons deadweight, delivered by Verolme, Heusden.
1978   William Robertson fleet, now reduced to nine vessels, was integrated with the Stephenson Clarke fleet from January 1, but "Gem" names retained.

SAPPHIRE   *L. Schofield*

Other activities such as brokerage, sale and purchase, chartering, freight forwarding distribution and agency work are carried on through Powell Duffryn Shipping Services Ltd., formed in 1976 to separate the group's shipowning interests from those services.

6

STEPHENSON CLARKE FLEET

FLEET LIST NOTES

The notation 'I', 'II' etc. in brackets after a ship's name indicates that she is the first, second, etc., ship of that name in the fleet. The dates following the name are those of entering and leaving the fleet, or coming under and leaving Stephenson Clarke ownership.

Ships are dry-cargo carriers unless otherwise noted. On the first line is given the ship's Official No. (O.N.) in the British registry, followed by her tonnages gross ('g'), nett ('n') and, where recorded, deadweight ('d'). These are followed by her dimensions — registered length x beam x depth in feet in tenths for ships numbered 1-63, and the overall length x beam x draught at summer deadweight for ships numbered 64-156, (incl. B.B.)=overall length including bulbous bow.

On the second line is given the type of engines and the name of the engine builders.'2-cyl. IDA' denotes a 2-cylinder inverted direct acting steam engine, 'C.2-cyl.'= Compound 2-cylinder and 'T.3-cyl'=triple expansion steam engines. For motor vessels, the number of cylinders in the engine is given and whether they are two stroke cycle (2 S.C.) or four stroke cycle (4 S.C.) single acting (S.A.) or double acting (D.A.). The indicated or brake horsepower (ihp or bhp) and speed is given for ships in the current fleet.

The ship's histories are corrected to February 1981.

1. J. M. STRACHAN (1865-1904)
ON. 52826. 762g, 518n, 199.8 × 28.1 × 17.4 feet
2-cyl. inverted direct acting steam engine by R. Stephenson & Co. Newcastle, replaced in 1882 by a 2-cyl. compound steam engine by J. Stewart & Son. Blackwall.
8.1865: Launched by Palmer Bros. & Co., Jarrow, Newcastle. *1882:* Re-engined. *12.1904:* Broken up at Harburg, Hamburg.

2. C. S. BUTLER (1865-1878)
ON. 54582. 760g, 517n, 199.7 × 28.1 × 17.4 feet
2-cyl. I.D.A. by R. Stephenson & Co., Newcastle.
8.1865: Launched by Palmer Brothers & Co., Jarrow. *20.12.1878:* Wrecked on Haisbro' Sands while on passage from the Tyne to London.

3. M. E. CLARKE (1865-1870)
ON. 54583. 656g, 509n, 180.6 × 28.0 × 17.0 feet
2-cyl. I.D.A. by R. Stephenson & Co., Newcastle.
10.1865: Launched by Palmer Brothers & Co., Jarrow. *19.11.1870:* Wrecked on Haisbro' Sands.

4. LORD ALFRED PAGET (1870-1892)
ON. 63680, 1870-1871: 866g, 574n, 223.5 × 28.2 × 17.3 feet
1871-on: 982g, 621n, 243.8 × 28.2 × 17.3 feet
2-cyl. I.D.A. by the Shipbuilders, compounded in 1885.
9.1870: Launched by Palmer's Shipbuilding & Iron Co. Ltd., Jarrow, Newcastle. *1871:* Lengthened 20.3 feet. *1892:* Sold to Wm. Cory & Son, registered under the ownership of C. F. Cory-Wright (J. Fenwick & Sons, managers) and renamed EASTWOOD. *1896:* Transferred to Wm. Cory & Son Ltd., London. *1910:* Broken up at Rotterdam by G. B. Pas & Zonen.

5. AGNES & LOUISA (1871-1881)
ON. 65675. 703g, 436n, 184.1 × 28.3 × 15.6 feet
C.2-cyl. by Black, Hawthorn & Co., Gateshead.
9.1871: Launched by Withy, Alexander & Co., West Hartlepool. *1881:* Sold to Jacob Lohden, West Hartlepool. *1888:* Sold to Agnes & Louisa Shares Co. Ltd., (Walker, Donald & Co., managers) London and renamed LUCHANA. *2.1.1893:* Wrecked near Cap la Hague while on a voyage from Glasgow to Cherbourg.

6. SHOREHAM (I) (1872-1888)
ON. 68361. 491g, 293n, 159.2 × 28.8 × 13.8 feet
C.2-cyl. by Walker, Henderson & Co., Glasgow.
8.1872: Launched by McFadyen & Co., Port Glasgow. *8.1.1888:* Sank after colliding with COLSTRUP, 506/74-s.s. off Kentish Knock Light Vessel while on passage from Shoreham to the Tyne in ballast.

7. LUIS DE CUADRA (1875)
ON. 73549. 923g, 596n, 210.5 × 29.3 × 15.4 feet
C.2-cyl. by J. Dickinson, Sunderland.
7.1875: Launched by R. Thompson, Jnr., Sunderland. *9.1875:* Sold to Segovia, Cuadra & Co., Spain. *1891:* Owners became Cia Sevillana de Nav. à Vapore, Spain. *1906:* Sold to Nicolaides Freres & V. Cokkins, Turkey and renamed HERMES. *1913:* Broken up.

ERASMUS WILSON in Thames Haven in 4.1897 with the bow of NEWBURN in the foreground. The latter's funnel and mast can be seen on the right of the picture

National Maritime Museum P.12014

8. ERASMUS WILSON (1876-1905)
ON. 73653. 805g, 497n, 199.0 × 30.1 × 18.2 feet
C.2-cyl. by Blair & Co. Ltd., Stockton.
3.1876: Launched by E. Withy & Co., West Hartlepool. *7.4.1897:* Collided at Thames Haven with NEWBURN, 680/61-s.s., which sank. *16.10.1905:* Sold to Watts, Watts & Co., London and renamed NEWMARKET. *1906:* Sold to Settsu Shosen Goshi Kaisha, Japan and renamed SUMINO-O MARU. *1908:* Sold to S. Tanaka, Japan. *1917:* Sold to H. Kaminade, Japan. *1920:* Sold to Hanji Magosaiji, Japan. *1924:* Sold to Obayashi Kenshiro, Japan. *1926:* Sold to Hamada Umekichi, Japan. *12.6.1927:* Sank following collision at the entrance to Tsugaru Strait.

9. LAFFITTE (1877-1878)
ON. 77070. 977g, 634n, 210.4 × 29.5 × 16.0 feet
C.2-cyl. by J. Dickinson, Sunderland.
12.1877: Launched by R. Thompson, Jnr., Sunderland. *2.1878:* Sold to Segovia, Cuadra & Co., Spain. *1891:* Owners became Cia Sevillana de Nav. à Vap., Spain. *1909:* Sold to G. Speranza & Co., Greece and renamed OMIROS. *1912:* Sold to G. Gaetanos, Turkey and renamed HUDAVENDIGHIAR. *1933:* Broken up.

10. GRACIE (1879-1900)
ON. 81587. 1312g, 811n, 261.0 × 32.1 × 17.0 feet
C.2-cyl. by Blair & Co. Ltd., Stockton.
9.1879: Launched by E. Withy & Co., West Hartlepool. *1900:* Sold to Tyneside Line Ltd., (J. Ridley, Son & Tully, managers) Newcastle. *1911:* Sold to Caloutas Bros. & L. Fafalios, Greece and renamed ALEX KALOUTAS. *1913:* Owners became A. Caloutas & fils, Greece. *1924:* Sold to E. Xenios & Co., Greece and renamed ELENI XENIOU. *1931:* Renamed PROFITIS ELIAS. *1933:* Broken up in Italy.

11. SAN FERNANDO (1880)
ON. 82801. 977g, 634n, 210.4 × 29.5 × 16.1 feet
C.2-cyl. by J. Dickinson, Sunderland.
8.1880: Launched by R. Thompson, Jnr., Sunderland and immediately sold to Segovia, Cuadra & Co., Spain. *1891:* Owners became Cia Sevillana de Nav. à Vap., Spain. *1907:* Sold to Nav. Orientale (P. Pantaleon, manager) Greece and renamed SPARTI. *1922:* Owners became Navigation Pantaleon (P. Pantaleon fils) Greece. *1930:* Sold to Ahmet Nafiz & Hassan Basri, Turkey and renamed GERZI. *1931:* Sold to Haci Yakup Zade Ahmet ve Ski, Turkey. *1935:* Sold to Vapurculuk Turk Anonim Sirketi, Turkey and renamed GERZE. *30.10.1935:* Wrecked in the Black Sea off Anatolia.

JOHN GRAFTON *World Ship Photo Library*

12. JOHN GRAFTON (1883-1905)
ON. 89504. 592g, 367n, 158.0 × 28.8 × 13.8 feet
C.2-cyl. by the Shipbuilders.
11.1883: Launched by Palmer's Shipbuilding & Iron Co. Ltd., Jarrow. *28.7.1905:* Sold to R. R. Dickinson & Co., London. *6.9.1905:* Arrived off Kalfskoer, 18 miles from Jacobstad and later reported to be aground on a sandbank three miles from land. *8.9.1905:* Boarded by Customs Officers who found her to be abandoned but with several thousand rifles on board. Twenty minutes after they left the ship exploded and rifles and "many" cases of revolvers were later washed ashore on the Skjold islands. Subsequent examination by divers located cases of bombs and explosives in the wreck. It is reported that the ship was under the Dutch flag at the time of her loss, but her name was obliterated.

13. PORTSLADE (I) (1888-1908)
ON. 95457. 634g, 385n, 161.7 × 29.9 × 11.9 feet
C.2-cyl. by North Eastern Marine Engineering Co. Ltd., Sunderland.
8.1888: Completed by R. Thompson & Sons, Sunderland. *1908:* Sold to Oakley, Street & Co., London. *1913:* Sold to C. F. Capponi & A. Milazzi (Brajak & Arnerich managers). Trieste, Austria-Hungary and renamed ELVIRA ANTONIETTA. *6.6.1914:* Wrecked at Rimini on the east coast of Italy while on passage from Bari to Venice. The wreck was later dismantled.

PORTSLADE at Shoreham *World Ship Photo Library*

F. E. WEBB at Shoreham   *World Ship Photo Library*

14. F. E. WEBB (1891-1912)
ON. 99001. 585g, 340n, 161.7 × 29.9 × 13.7 feet
T.3-cyl. by North Eastern Marine Engineering Co. Ltd., Sunderland.
10.1891: Completed by R. Thompson & Sons, Sunderland. *1912:* Sold to Keeps S.S. &
Lighterage Co. Ltd., (H. Keep, manager) London. *1916:* Sold to Bargate Steam Shipping Co. Ltd.,
(F. A. Hobbs, manager) Grimsby, and renamed SCARTHO. *1923:* Sold to Rederi A/B Scartho (H.
Witt, manager) Sweden. *1933:* Sold to A. B. Carlsson, Sweden and renamed BIRMA. *2.3.1938:*
Abandoned at sea off Hirtshals while on passage from Gdynia to Selby and later sank.

15. ALICE V. GOODHUE (1892-1896) Wood brigantine
ON. 38149. 151g, 134n, 90.0 × 23.3 × 11 9 feet
1861: Launched at Salmon River, Nova Scotia for A. C. Robbins & E. C. Moulton, Yarmouth N.S.
7.1868: Sold to J. Stephens, Falmouth. *1877:* Sold to J. Creasy, Falmouth. *1884:* Sold to B.
Blaker, Shoreham. *1886:* Sold to T. P. Cattley, Shoreham. *1892:* Bought by Stephenson Clarke
& Co. *1896:* Sold to J. Robinson, Littlehampton. *1907:* Sold to A. B. Coles Ltd., London. *1911:*
Sold to J. Borrow and dismantled for use as a coal hulk.

16. CONFLICT (1892-1894) Wood snow
ON. 45738. 227g, 227n, 99.5 × 24.5 × 14.8 feet.
7.1864: Launched by H. Barrick, Whitby for his own account. *1869:* Sold to W. Banfield,
Shoreham. *1883:* Sold to W. Pannett, Newhaven. *1892:* Bought by Stephenson Clarke & Co.
21.12.1894: Sailed from Hartlepool for Shoreham and thereafter disappeared.

17. EBENEZER (1892-1895) Wood brig
ON. 27430. 177g, 177n, 108.7 × 22.5 × 11.4 feet
5.1860: Launched by May, Shoreham for W. Banfield, Shoreham. *1882:* Sold to T. P. Cattley,
Shoreham. *1892:* Bought by Stephenson Clarke & Co. *1895:* Sold to J. Robinson, Littlehampton.
15.7.1917: Intercepted by German submarine 25 miles N.W. of Dieppe and sunk by explosive
charges.

18. PROSPERO (1892-1899) Wood brig
ON. 13331. 144n, 88.7 × 21.9 × 12.4 feet
1856: Launched at Rye for Hessell & Co., Rye. *1865:* Sold to Fuller & Co., Rye. *1880:* Sold to G.
Molineux & Co., Rye. *1881:* Sold to B. Blaker, Shoreham. *8.1884:* Sold to T. P. Cattley,
Shoreham. *1892:* Bought by Stephenson Clarke & Co. *1.1899:* Sold to John Pattison, West
Hartlepool. *10.1.1903:* Wrecked near Mundesley while on passage from London to Hartlepool.

19. SARAH (1892-1896) Wood brig
ON. 44876. 185n, 110.0 × 23.0 × 11.6 feet
9.1862: Launched by May, Shoreham for W. Banfield, Shoreham. *1882:* Sold to T. P. Cattley,
Shoreham. *1892:* Bought by Stephenson Clark & Co. *1896:* Sold to J. Robinson, Littlehampton.
1910: Sold to T. C. Coverley & Co., transferred to Portuguese flag and hulked at Oporto.

10

20. ANDALUCIA (1892-1896)
1800g, 1160n, 250.0 × 36.0 × 16.8 feet
T.3-cyl. by North Eastern Marine Engineering Co. Ltd., Sunderland.
9.1892: Completed by R. Thompson & Sons, Sunderland and registered at Seville. *1896:* Sold to
Espaliu & Cia Spain. *1898:* Owners became Cia Anon. de Vap., Vinuesa, Spain. *1916:* Sold to
Cia Trasmediterranea, Spain. *1936:* Broken up.

21. ST. DUNSTAN (1892-1911)
ON. 101937. 1014g, 619n, 220.0 × 31.0 × 14.0 feet
T.3-cyl. by North Eastern Marine Engineering Co. Ltd., Sunderland.
10.1892: Completed by S. P. Austin & Son, Sunderland. *1911:* Sold to G. E. Salvagno, Italy and
renamed CARLO ZENO. *1913:* Owners became G. E. Salvagno & Nipoti, Italy. *1923:* Owners
became G. & E. Salvagno, Italy. *1924:* Sold to Ern. Milano fu A., Italy and renamed MIRONE.
1929: Sold to E. Matkovic, Yugoslavia and renamed LJUBICA. *1930:* Renamed LJUBICA
MATKOVIC. *1937:* Sold to George J. Pappayanakis, Greece and renamed KATINA P. II. *1939:*
Sold to Mme. A. A. Davaris & P. H. Tzanetatos, Greece and renamed ANTIKLIA, *Subsequently*
the owner became P. H. Tzanetatos, Greece. *1949:* Sold to Antiklia Chryssoverghi, Greece.
1951: Sold to P. E. Baikas, Greece and renamed ASSIMINA. *1953:* Broken up in Italy.

22. RALPH (1895-1903)
ON. 105733. 184g, 74n, 110.0 × 20.0 × 8.0 feet
C.2-cyl. by North Eastern Marine Engineering Co. Ltd., Sunderland.
9.1895: Completed by R. Thompson & Sons, Sunderland. *1903:* Sold to Scotto, Ambrosino &
Pugliese, France and renamed VILLE DE MOSTAGANEM. *1911:* Sold to Soc. di Nav. à Vap.,
Liguria Occidentale, Italy and renamed LIGURIA. *12.1919:* Wrecked in the Black Sea near
Odessa whilst on a voyage from Odessa to Caspoli.

23. LEWIS (I) (1897-1902)
ON. 108265. 196g, 77n, 115.0 × 20.1 × 9.0 feet
C.2-cyl. by North Eastern Marine Engineering Co. Ltd., Sunderland.
11.1897: Completed by R. Thompson & Sons, Sunderland. *1902:* Sold to Menendez y
Fernandez, Spain and renamed ASTURIAS. *1907:* Owner became R. Fernandez, Spain. *1910:*
Sold to F. Garcia, Spain and renamed GARCIA No. 2. *1919:* Renamed PACO GARCIA. *1923:*
Sold to Vapores Costeros S.A., Spain. *29.12.1959:* Foundered six miles off Cape Vidio, near
Gijon during a gale while on passage from Gijon to Burela.

24. ST. AGNES (1903-1925)
ON. 118316. 1195g, 740n, 227.8 × 35.1 × 14.6 feet
T.3-cyl. by North Eastern Marine Engineering Co. Ltd., Sunderland.
8.1903: Completed by S. P. Austin & Son Ltd., Sunderland. *1925:* Sold to M. Goossens, Belgium
and renamed RIP. *9.1936:* Arrived at Newport, Mon., to be broken up by John Cashmore & Co.
Ltd.

25. LEWIS (II) (1903-1912)
ON. 118322. 346g, 139n, 135.0 × 24.2 × 10.5 feet
T.3-cyl. by North Eastern Marine Engineering Co. Ltd., Sunderland.
9.1903: Completed by Wood, Skinner & Co. Ltd., Newcastle. *1912:* Sold to Care & Young Ltd.,
Cardiff. *1912:* Resold to Thos. W. Ward Ltd., Sheffield by whom she was, in *1939,* broken up at
Briton Ferry.

LEWIS (II) *World Ship Photo Library*

11

26. EDDIE (1904-1910)
ON. 118447. 219g, 86n, 115.0 × 20.1 × 9.0 feet
C.2-cyl. by North Eastern Marine Engineering Co. Ltd., Newcastle. Re-engined in 1933 with a 6-cyl. 4SCSA oil engine by W. H. Allen, Sons & Co. Ltd., Bedford.
6.1904: Completed by Wood, Skinner & Co. Ltd., Newcastle. *1910:* Sold to J. S. Cole, Newcastle. *1922:* Sold to Moorcroft Shipping Co. Ltd., (Robert Owen & Co., managers) Liverpool. *1931:* Sold to Colonial Lands Improvement Co. Ltd., Jersey. *1933:* Sold to Union Drydock & Engineering Co. Ltd., Hull and converted to a motor vessel. *12.10.1934:* Wrecked off Goole.

ST. EDMUND as MIERVALDIS   *World Ship Photo Library*

27. ST. EDMUND (1904-1922)
ON. 120461. 1228g, 758n, 234.6 × 36.1 × 14.9 feet
T.3-cyl. by the Shipbuilders.
10.1904: Completed by Clyde Shipbuilding & Engineering Co. Ltd., Port Glasgow. *1922:* Sold to Kingsdon Steamship Co. Ltd., Cardiff and renamed KINGSDON. *1929:* Sold to Stahl & Co. (D. Thomsons, manager) Latvia and renamed MIERVALDIS. *15.10.1940:* Taken over by the Ministry of War Transport, registered at Swansea and placed under the management of Broomhill Steamships Ltd., Newcastle. *1948:* Hudson S.S. Co. Ltd., appointed managers. *17.7.1948:* Laid up and then loaded with a cargo of poison gas. *22.9.1948:* Scuttled in the Bay of Biscay. She carried 1880 tons of chemical warfare ammunition and was the last of seventeen obsolete ships sunk after the war with this type of cargo aboard.

28. BROOK (1906-1919)
ON. 120682. 1436g, 891n. 248.0 × 36.3 × 15.9 feet
T.3-cyl. by G. Clark Ltd., Sunderland.
3.1906: Completed by S. P. Austin & Son Ltd., Sunderland. *2.5.1919:* Transferred to Brentford Gas Company, remaining under Stephenson Clarke management. *10.2.1924:* Sunk in collision 2½ miles from the Shipwash Light Vessel, while on passage from the Tyne to London.

29. SOFIE (1907-1918)
ON. 125640. 354g, 138n, 135.0 × 24.2 × 10.6 feet
T.3-cyl. by North Eastern Marine Engineering Co. Ltd., Sunderland.
11.1907: Completed by Wood, Skinner & Co. Ltd., Newcastle. *31.3.1917:* Attacked by gunfire from a German submarine when in the English Channel. *3.2.1918:* Torpedoed and sunk by U.101 South of Milford Haven while on passage from Jersey to Cardiff. Eight members of her crew including the Master were lost.

30. JOHN MILES (1908-1917)
ON. 125659. 687g, 342n, 164.0 × 30.0 × 11.9 feet
T.3-cyl. by North Eastern Marine Engineering Co. Ltd., Sunderland.
1.1908: Completed by S. P. Austin & Son Ltd., Sunderland. *22.2.1917:* Torpedoed 11 miles S.E. from Hartlepool by UB21 and sank with the loss of 10 lives including the Master. She was on a voyage from the Tyne to Shoreham.

CORBET WOODALL

31. CORBET WOODALL (1908-1917)
ON. 125712. 917g, 544n, 200.1 × 33.0 × 12.5 feet
T.3-cyl. by North Eastern Marine Engineering Co. Ltd., Sunderland.
7.1908: Completed by S. P. Austin & Son Ltd., Sunderland. *30.5.1917:* Mined and sank $1\frac{1}{2}$ miles east from the Nab Light Vessel, while on passage from the Tyne to Poole with coal. The mine had been laid by UC.36.

REGIS, in John Kelly Ltd colours

32. REGIS (1909-1932)
ON. 129038. 1370g, 798n, 235.1 × 36.1 × 15.5 feet
T.3-cyl. by North Eastern Marine Engineering Co. Ltd., Sunderland.
9.1909: Completed by S. P. Austin & Son Ltd., Sunderland. *1932:* Transferred to John Kelly Ltd., Belfast. *1935:* Sold to Tallinn Shipping Co. Ltd., Estonia and renamed OLEV. *13.10.1940:* Taken over by the Ministry of Shipping (later Ministry of War Transport) re-registered at Belfast and placed under the management of France, Fenwick Tyne & Wear Co. Ltd., London. *1942:* Tyne & Wear Shipping Co. Ltd., appointed managers. *1949:* Management transferred by Ministry of Transport to W. A. Souter & Co. Ltd. *1950:* Sold to Cia. Mar. Labaro S.A., Panama (A/B H. Neuhaus & Co. — successors to Tallinn Shipping Co. Ltd., managers) and renamed LABARO. *1.2.1957:* Arrived at Antwerp for demolition at Willebroeck by L. Engelen.

SEAFORD (I)

Courtesy R. Fenton

33. SEAFORD (I) (1911-1934)
ON. 129200. 673g, 349n, 164.5 × 30.0 × 12.1 feet
T.3-cyl. by North Eastern Marine Engineering Co. Ltd., Newcastle.
5.1911: Completed by W. Dobson & Co., Newcastle. *1934:* Sold to A. F. Henry & MacGregor Ltd., Leith and renamed TOLSTA HEAD. *1946:* Sold to H. P. Lenaghan, Belfast and renamed BANTRY BAY. *1947:* Sold to Th. Larsen, Denmark and renamed MARY STON. *1949:* Lengthened 30 feet to 194.5 feet, tonnages now 813g, 447n. *1950:* Sold to Fellow Steamship Co. Inc., Liberia. *4.6.1953:* Arrived at Antwerp for demolition by Omer Bulens who began work 21.9.1953.

MINSTER (I)

World Ship Photo Library

34. MINSTER (I) (1911-1914)
ON. 132573. 2788g, 1686n, 314.0 × 45.7 × 20.9 feet
T.3-cyl. by North Eastern Marine Engineering Co. Ltd., Sunderland.
7.1911: Completed by S. P. Austin & Son Ltd., Sunderland. *4.8.1914:* Sold to W. J. Tillett S.S. Co. Ltd., (W. J. Tillett & Co., managers), Cardiff and renamed ROSEHILL. *23.9.1917:* Torpedoed and sunk by UB40 five miles S.W. by S. from Fowey while on passage from Cardiff to Devonport. The wreck was later sold to Roy Davis of Bodmin.

ABBAS (I)   *World Ship Photo Library*

35. ABBAS (I) (1911-1935)
ON. 132628. 1430g, 836n, 240.0 × 36.0 × 15.6 feet
T.3-cyl. by J. Dickinson & Sons Ltd., Sunderland.
11.1911: Completed by S. P. Austin & Son Ltd., Sunderland. *1935:* Sold to Mme K. G. Sigalas, (G. Sigalas Sons, managers) Greece and renamed KADIO. *23.10.1941:* Sank following explosion in Suez Roads.

COMBE   *World Ship Photo Library*

36. COMBE (1912-1915)
ON. 135180. 2030g, 1222n, 275.2 × 39.0 × 18.6 feet
T.3-cyl. by J. Dickinson & Sons Ltd., Sunderland.
12.1912: Completed by Wood, Skinner & Co. Ltd., Newcastle. *27.4.1915-25.9.1915:* Served as Collier No. 662. *26.9.1915:* Ammunition Carrier for Russian Government account. *12.10.1915:* Sailed from Liverpool for Archangel. *14.10.1915:* Parted from her escort and thereafter disappeared. *29.12.1915:* Posted missing.

37. CERNE (I) (1915-1916)
ON. 136755. 2579g, 1493n, 315.0 × 45.0 × 19.3 feet
T.3-cyl. by G. Clark Ltd., Sunderland.
1.1915: Completed by S. P. Austin & Son Ltd., Sunderland. *26.3.1916:* Mined and sank four miles N.E. from Elbow Buoy while on passage from the Tyne to London with coal. The mine had been laid by UC7.

KEYNES (I) *Brownell Collection*

38. KEYNES (I) (1915-1940)
ON. 136810. 1706g, 1021n, 260.1 × 37.7 × 16.4 feet
T.3-cyl. by North Eastern Marine Engineering Co. Ltd., Newcastle.
3.1915: Completed by Wood, Skinner & Co., Ltd., Newcastle. *11.1.1940:* Sunk by air attack East of Hornsea in a position 53.47N, 0.46E while on passage from Southampton to Sunderland. Her crew was saved.

> **AUBE (1916-1917)** — See N.1 below.
> **SOMME (1916-1917)** — See N.2 below.

J. B. PADDON *Author's Collection*

39. J. B. PADDON (1917-1941)
ON. 137147. 570g, 250n, 175.6 × 27.0 × 10.4 feet
T.3-cyl. by Lidgerwood, Ltd., Glasgow.
7.1914: Completed by Ardrossan Dry Dock & Shipbuilding Co. Ltd., Ardrossan as STARBEAM for North British Shipowners Ltd., (G. Elsmie & Son, managers) Aberdeen. *1917:* Bought by Stephenson Clarke & Co., and renamed J. B. PADDON. *27.12.1941:* Sank following air attack East of Hornsea in a position 53.55N, 0.16E while on passage from Lowestoft to Seaham. Her crew was saved.

40. HOVE (1917-1935)

ON. 133629. 435g, 170n, 155.8 × 25.2 × 10.8 feet
T.3-cyl. by W. V. V. Lidgerwood, Glasgow.
7.1913: Completed by Ardrossan Dry Dock & Shipbuilding Co. Ltd., Ardrossan as COLLAIRNIE for North British Shipowners Ltd., (G. Elsmie & Son, managers) Aberdeen. *1917:* Bought by Stephenson Clarke & Co., and renamed HOVE. *1935:* Sold to Coppack Bros. & Co., Connah's Quay. *23.6.1961:* Arrived at Dublin for demolition by Hammond Lane Metal Co. Ltd., who began work 1.7.1961.

> **BELTOY (1918-1923)** — See N.3 below.
> **GRANSHA (1918-1923)** — See N.4 below.
> **GLYNN (1918-1923)** — See N.5 below.
> **MOYLE (1918-1923)** — See N.6 below.
> **TROSTAN (1918-1920)** — See N.7 below.
> **VAUX (1920-1925)** — See N.8 below.
> **LYS (1920-1925)** — See N.9 below.

41. BORDE (I) (1921-1940)

ON. 145167. 2014g, 1099n, 270.4 × 38.2 × 18.5 feet
T.3-cyl. by North Eastern Marine Engineering Co. Ltd., Sunderland.
3.1921: Completed by John Crown & Sons Ltd., Sunderland. *18.10.1939:* Requisitioned and *28.10.1939* purchased, by the Admiralty for service as a Mine Destructor Vessel and commissioned as H.M.S. BORDE. *7.1942:* Completed conversion to a Maintenance and Repair Ship for Minesweepers. *11.4.1945:* Handed over to British Iron & Steel Corporation (Salvage) Ltd., at Swansea and allocated to T. W. Ward Ltd., but foundered on passage to Milford Haven.

> **ANDELLE (1922-1925)** — See N.10 below.
> **NIVELLE (1923-1925)** — See N.11 below.

LANCING (I)   *G. A. Osbon*

42. LANCING (I) (1923-1933)

ON. 124393. 703g, 278n, 182.7 × 27.9 × 12.3 feet
T.3-cyl. by Ross & Duncan, Glasgow.
3.1908: Completed by R. Williamson & Son, Workington as RAVONIA for their own account. *1915:* Sold to Commercial Gas Co., London. *1919:* Sold to Wandsworth, Wimbledon & Epsom District Gas Co. *1923:* Bought by Stephenson Clarke & Co. Ltd., and renamed LANCING. *1933:* Sold to G. Balzano, (later G. Balzano fu Achille) Italy and renamed GIANNINA. *1935:* Sold to Giuseppe Agrifoglio, Italy and renamed ALVERNIA. *1936:* Sold to F. Italo Croce, Italy and renamed RINA CROCE. *1937:* Sold to Alberto Maria Volpe, Italy and renamed GIGLIOLA. *1939:* Sold to Mario Veronesi, Italy. *9.1943:* Seized by German authorities. *8.2.1944:* Sunk at Zara by Allied air attack.

43. ASHLEY (I) (1924-1940)

ON. 147616. 1323g, 716n, 235.0 × 35.6 × 14.7 feet
T.3-cyl. by North Eastern Marine Engineering Co. Ltd., Newcastle.
4.1924: Completed by Wood, Skinner & Co. Ltd., Newcastle. *9.3.1940:* Wrecked $\frac{1}{2}$ mile South of North Goodwin Light Vessel while on passage from Sunderland to Southampton.

ASHLEY (I) *Alex Duncan*

44. MATCHING (1924-1955)
ON. 147705. 1321g, 715n, 235.0 × 35.6 × 14.8 feet
T.3-cyl. by J. Dickinson & Sons Ltd., Sunderland.
8.1924: Completed by John Crown & Sons Ltd., Sunderland. *7.4.1955:* Delivered to British Iron & Steel Corporation (Salvage) Ltd., and allocated to Clayton & Davie Ltd. *8.4.1955:* Arrived at their Dunston on Tyne yard for demolition.

MATCHING (with Gerald Brownell's "Green Goddess" alongside) *World Ship Photo Library*

45. WILLIAM CASH (1929-1958)
ON. 161303. 1186g, 681n, 225.5 × 36.1 × 14.0 feet
T.3-cyl. by North Eastern Marine Engineering Co. Ltd., Sunderland.
9.1929: Completed by R. & W. Hawthorn, Leslie & Co. Ltd., Newcastle. *7.9.1940:* Sank in Royal Victoria Dock, London when a German bomb went through her during an air raid. *16.9.1940:* Drydocked for repairs. *4.4.1958:* Arrived in the New Waterway in tow of the tug GUARDSMAN bound for Krimpen a/d Ijssel for demolition by Metaalhandel en Sloopwerken H. P. Heuvelman.

ILSE (1929-1942) — See M.1 below.

18

WILLIAM CASH   *T. Rayner*

46. FLATHOUSE (1931-1961)
ON. 162665. 1546g, 837n, 244.0 × 36.5 × 16.0 feet
T.3-cyl. by the Shipbuilders' Newcastle works.
12.1931: Completed by Swan, Hunter & Wigham Richardson Ltd., Sunderland. *16.2.1961:*
Arrived at Grays, Essex, for demolition by Thos. W. Ward Ltd.

FLATHOUSE   *World Ship Photo Library*

47. PITWINES (1932-1941)
ON. 146694. 932g, 535n, 209.3 × 31.4 × 13.3 feet
T.3-cyl. by North Eastern Marine Engineering Co. Ltd., Newcastle.
1.1923: Completed by Burntisland Shipbuilding Co. Ltd., Burntisland as WANDLE for
Wandsworth, Wimbledon & Epsom District Gas Co., London. *1931:* Owner's name became
Wandsworth & District Gas Co. *1932:* Bought by Stephenson Clarke & Associated Companies
Ltd., and renamed PITWINES. *19.11.1941:* Sank after colliding off Hartlepool with GATESHEAD,
744/19 - s.s. while on passage from Middlesbrough to London.

PITWINES   *Brownell Collection*

PULBOROUGH (I)   G. A. Osbon

48. PULBOROUGH (I) (1933-1940)
ON. 163383. 960g, 524n, 205.0 × 33.0 × 13.1 feet
T.3-cyl. by D. Rowan & Co. Ltd., Glasgow.
9.1933: Completed by Burntisland Shipbuilding Co. Ltd., Burntisland. *20.7.1940:* Sunk by air attack two miles off Dover Pier while on passage from the Tyne to Shoreham. Her crew was saved.

SIR RUSSELL   Alex Duncan

49. SIR RUSSELL (1933-1941)
ON. 163408. 1548g, 841n, 243.8 × 36.6 × 16.1 feet
T.3-cyl. by the Shipbuilders.
11.1933: Completed by Swan, Hunter & Wigham Richardson Ltd., Newcastle. *11.8.1941:* Sunk by E-boat 6½ miles E.N.E. of Dungeness while on passage from the Wear to Southampton. Her crew was saved.

50. CERNE (II) (1934-1955)
ON. 147672. 1257g, 670n, 220.7 × 34.9 × 16.4 feet
T.3-cyl. by North Eastern Marine Engineering Co. Ltd., Newcastle.
5.1924: Completed by Burntisland Shipbuilding Co. Ltd., Burntisland as WOODCOTE for Wandsworth, Wimbledon & Epsom District Gas Co., London. *1931:* Owner's name became Wandsworth & District Gas Co. *1934:* Bought by Stephenson Clarke & Associated Companies Ltd., and renamed CERNE. *1955:* Sold to British Iron & Steel Corporation (Salvage) Ltd., and allocated to Clayton & Davie Ltd. *27.7.1955:* Arrived at their Dunston on Tyne yard for demolition.

PETWORTH (I)   *G. A. Osbon*

51. PETWORTH (I) (1934-1957)
ON. 163512. 972g, 518n, 205.0 × 33.0 × 13.1 feet
T.3-cyl. by D. Rowan & Co. Ltd., Glasgow.
8.1934: Completed by Burntisland Shipbuilding Co. Ltd., Burntisland. *1957:* Sold to Onesimus
Dorey & Sons Ltd., Guernsey and renamed BELVEDERE. *22.8.1960:* Arrived at Nieuw Lekkerkerk
for demolition by Machinehandel en Scheepssloperij "De Koophandel".

HENRY WOODALL   *Brownell Collection*

52. HENRY WOODALL (1935-1940)
ON. 164539. 625g, 270n, 177.0 × 27.6 × 10.9 feet
T.3-cyl. by North Eastern Marine Engineering Co. Ltd., Sunderland.
1935: Completed by R. & W. Hawthorn, Leslie & Co. Ltd., Newcastle. *10.5.1940:* Mined and
sunk three miles East of Withernsea while on passage from Great Yarmouth to Seaham. Six of
her crew of 12 and one of the two gunners were lost.

53. HORSTED (I) (1936-1939)
ON. 164707. 1670g, 932n, 256.0 × 37.5 × 16.4 feet
T.3-cyl. by D. Rowan & Co. Ltd., Glasgow.
9.1936: Completed by Burntisland Shipbuilding Co. Ltd., Burntisland. *4.12.1939:* Sank S.E. of
Flamborough Head in a position 53.48N, 0.16E after striking a mine while on passage from
London to Sunderland. Five of her crew were lost.

21

54. PORTSLADE (II) (1936-1940)
ON. 164721. 1091g, 620n, 210.5 × 33.2 × 14.0 feet
T.3-cyl. by North Eastern Marine Engineering Co. Ltd., Sunderland.
9.1936: Completed by William Pickersgill & Sons Ltd., Sunderland. *25.7.1940:* Sunk by air attack off Sandgate while on passage from Sunderland to Shoreham. Her crew of 17 was saved.

ELEANOR BROOKE   *Skyfotos*

55. ELEANOR BROOKE (1938-1957)
ON. 166370. 1037g, 571n, 211.3 × 34.2 × 13.4 feet
T.3-cyl. by North Eastern Marine Engineering Co. Ltd., Sunderland.
3.1938: Completed by S. P. Austin & Son Ltd., Sunderland. *1957:* Sold to Kristian E. Samuelsen, Norway and renamed SVELGEN. *1963:* Sold to Sligtransport A/S (K. E. Samuelsen manager) Norway. *1963:* Sold to A. Stokkas Rederi A/S (Anders Stokka, manager) Norway. *1964:* Renamed STOKKVIK. *1964:* Re-engined with a 7-cyl. 2SCSA oil engine by Wichmann Motorfabrikk A/L, Rubbestadneset. *1968:* Sold to A/S Anjo & others (Johan Ystas, manager) Norway. *1970:* Sold to K/S A/S Sira & Co., (Brodrene Klovning, manager) Norway and renamed SIRAVIK. *1973:* Sold to Per Opem, Norway and renamed ANNE OPEM. *1974:* Sold to Star Seal Shipping Co. S.A., Panama and renamed MONIA. *1977:* Sold to Yeslam-Salem-Alshagga, Panama. Still in service.

ELIZABETH LYSAGHT   *G. A. Osbon*

56. ELIZABETH LYSAGHT (1938-1958)
ON. 166439. 1037g, 572n, 211.3 × 34.2 × 13.4 feet
T.3-cyl. by North Eastern Marine Engineering Co. Ltd., Sunderland.
5.1938: Completed by S. P. Austin & Son Ltd., Sunderland. *1958:* Sold to Francesco Esposito, Italy and renamed RINO ESPOSITO. *1.1960:* Re-engined with an 8-cyl. 4SCSA oil engine by Maschinenwerke Kiel. *1961:* Sold to Cesare Giovagnoni, Italy and renamed ZAFFIRO. *1962:* Sold to Lighea di Nav., S.p.A., Italy. *1964:* Sold to Michele Scotto di Mase, Italy. *12.5.1970:* Found abandoned and wrecked off Cap Bengut, Algeria. Her crew was subsequently found. She had been on a voyage from Nemur to Olbia.

SYLVIA BEALE at Shoreham   *G. A. Osbon*

57. SYLVIA BEALE (1938-1960)
ON. 166480. 1040g, 572n, 211.3 × 34.2 × 13.4 feet
T.3-cyl. by North Eastern Marine Engineering Co. Ltd., Sunderland.
6.1938: Completed by S. P. Austin & Son Ltd., Sunderland. *1960:* Sold to British Iron & Steel Corporation (Salvage) Ltd., and allocated to Clayton & Davie Ltd., who began work at Dunston in 7.1960.

58. BROADHURST (I) (1939-1940)
ON. 164882. 1013g, 567n, 217.0 × 34.0 × 12.5 feet
T.3-cyl. by North Eastern Marine Engineering Co. Ltd., Sunderland.
11.1935: Completed by S. P. Austin & Son Ltd., as PHYLWOOD for Wm. France, Fenwick & Co. Ltd., London. *1939:* Bought by Stephenson Clarke & Associated Companies Ltd., and renamed BROADHURST. *26.7.1940:* Sunk by E-boat 14 miles S. × W. of Shoreham during a voyage from Seaham to Shoreham. Four of her crew were lost.

59. NEPHRITE/PORTSLADE (III) (1939-1954)
ON. 149917. 927g, 493n, 199.7 × 30.9 × 12.7 feet
T.3-cyl. by the Shipbuilders.
10.1927: Completed by John Lewis & Sons Ltd., Aberdeen as BURSTOW for Edward T. Lindley, London. *1932:* Sold to William Robertson, Glasgow and renamed NEPHRITE. *1939:* Bought by Stephenson Clarke & Associated Companies Ltd. *8.9.1942:* Attacked and damaged by German aircraft $4\frac{1}{2}$ miles East of Ramsgate while on passage from Shoreham to the Tyne. *9.3.1945:* While on Government service at Granville attacked by a German raiding party who set the ship on fire and killed three of her crew and the gunner. *1946:* Renamed PORTSLADE. *1954:* Sold to Ouse S.S. Co. Ltd., (E. P. Atkinson & Sons, managers) Goole and renamed ROSEFLEET. *29.10.1956:* Stranded during a gale at Mardyck 3 miles West of Dunkirk while on passage from Dunkirk to Goole in ballast. *12.1956:* Broken up as she lay by M. Vincent, Liege.

PORTSLADE (III)   *World Ship Photo Library*

60. BETTY HINDLEY (I) (1941)

ON. 168202. 1738g, 922n, 258.0 × 38.3 × 16.6 feet
T.3-cyl. by North Eastern Marine Engineering Co. (1938) Ltd., Sunderland.
7.1941: Completed by S. P. Austin & Son Ltd., Sunderland. *6.8.1941:* Wrecked on Haisbro'
Sand, in a position 52.54.30 N, 1.43.30 E, while on passage from the Tyne to London.

BETTY HINDLEY (II) *Alex Duncan*

61. BETTY HINDLEY (II) (1943-1947)

ON. 168375. 1771g, 955n, 258.0 × 38.3 × 16.6 feet
T.3-cyl. by North Eastern Marine Engineering Co. (1938) Ltd., Sunderland.
1.1943: Completed by S. P. Austin & Son Ltd., Sunderland. *7.10.1947:* Struck a mine 3 miles
East of Scarborough during a ballast voyage from London to the Tyne. Whilst being towed in
8.10.1947 she sank 1½ miles S.E. of Scarborough Castle.

62. BOWCOMBE (I) (1943-1946, 1949-1966)

ON. 168412. 2760g, 1533n, 311.4 × 44.5 × 19.3 feet
T.3-cyl. by North Eastern Marine Engineering (Co. (1938) Ltd., Sunderland.
4.1943: Completed by S. P. Austin & Son, Ltd., Sunderland. *1946:* Sold to Coastwise Colliers
Ltd., (Wm. France, Fenwick & Co. Ltd., managers) London. *1946:* Renamed COLWYN. *1949:*
Repurchased by Stephenson Clarke, Ltd.. and renamed BOWCOMBE. *1966:* Sold to Skrot &
Avfallsprodukter and converted into a lighter for Torsten Johannisson, Sweden.

ROGATE (II) *World Ship Photo Library*

63. ROGATE (I) (1944-1945)
ON. 169928. 2871g, 1602n, 317.3 × 44.5 × 19.9 feet
T.3-cyl. by North Eastern Marine Engineering Co. (1938) Ltd., Sunderland.
7.1944: Completed by S. P. Austin & Son Ltd., Sunderland. *19.3.1945:* Sunk by E-boat off Lowestoft while on passage from Sunderland to London. Two members of her crew were lost.

64. ROGATE (II) (1946-1964)
ON. 180087. 2849g, 1569n, 4140d. 321'1" × 44'5" × 19'4½"
T.3-cyl. by Central Marine Engine Works, West Hartlepool.
3.1946: Completed by Wm. Gray & Co. Ltd., West Hartlepool as EMPIRE GOWER for the Ministry of Transport (Weidner, Hopkins & Co., managers). *24.4.1946:* Bought by Stephenson Clarke Ltd., and renamed ROGATE. *1964:* Sold to Aghia Barbara Cia. Mar. S.A., Panama and renamed SANTA BARBARA. *2.11.1971:* Laid up at Piraeus. *8.8.1972:* Ch. Christodoulou and A. Bokas commenced demolition at Perama.

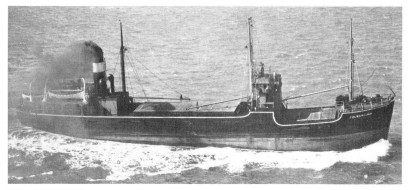

PULBOROUGH (II)   *Skyfotos*

65. PULBOROUGH (II)/PULBOROUGH II (1946-1959)
ON. 180991. 1047g, 569n, 1441d. 212'0" × 32'10" × 15'2½"
T.3-cyl. by the Shipbuilders.
8.1945: Completed by John Lewis & Sons Ltd., Aberdeen as EMPIRE RICHMOND for the Ministry of War Transport (O. Dorey & Sons Ltd., managers). *1946:* Sold to Stephenson Clarke Ltd., and renamed PULBOROUGH. *1959:* Renamed PULBOROUGH II. *1959:* Sold to M. P. Kurian, India and renamed NILGIRI. *20.4.1970:* India Metal Traders began demolition at Calcutta.

KEYNES (II)   *World Ship Photo Library*

66. KEYNES (II) (1946-1966)
ON. 180839. 1563g, 826n, 2230d. 269'11" × 36'6" × 16'10¼"
T.3-cyl. by North Eastern Marine Engineering Co. (1938) Ltd., Sunderland.
3.1946: Completed by S. P. Austin & Son Ltd., Sunderland. *1966:* Sold to Torsten Johannisson, Sweden and renamed GRANITA IV. *3.7.1969:* Broken up at Gothenburg.

   PORTSLADE (III) (1946-1954) — See NEPHRITE, No. 59, above.

67. ASHLEY (II) (1947-1957)
ON. 164885. 1067g, 532n, 1350d. 227'6" × 34'0" × 13'11"
T.3-cyl. by North Eastern Marine Engineering Co. Ltd., Sunderland.
7.1936: Completed by Wm. Pickersgill & Sons Ltd., Sunderland as BETSWOOD for Wm. France, Fenwick & Co. Ltd., London. *1946:* Registered under Shoreham Shipping & Coal Co. Ltd. *1947:* Bought by Stephenson Clarke Ltd. *1957:* Sold to Onesimus Dorey & Sons Ltd., Guernsey and renamed HAVELET. *2.10.1961:* Arrived at Terneuzen for demolition by N. V. Scheldeveen.

68. SEAFORD (II) (1947-1971)
ON. 181770. 1108g, 559n, 1510d. 225'0" × 34'6" × 14'7½"
6-cyl. 2SCSA oil engine by British Polar Engines Ltd., Glasgow.
— The first motor vessel in the fleet —
11.1947: Completed by S. P. Austin & Son Ltd., Sunderland. *1971:* Sold to Efti Shipping Co. Ltd., Cyprus and renamed CICILIANA. *1972:* Sold to P. Alogoskoufis, Greece and renamed GEORGIOS A. Still in service.

BRANKSOME   *Brownell Collection*

69. BRANKSOME (1948-1962)
ON. 181832. 1438g, 733n, 1905d. 253'0" × 36'8" × 15'7¾"
T.3-cyl. by North Eastern Marine Engineering Co. (1938) Ltd., Sunderland.
2.1948: Completed by S. P. Austin & Son Ltd., Sunderland. *1962:* Sold to Floramar Cia. di Nav., Italy and renamed ZAGARA. *1964:* Sold to Silvio Bonaso, Italy and renamed PINETTA. *1966:* Sold to African Shipping & Trading Co. Ltd., Liberia and renamed TJRA. *23.5.1969:* Arrived at Bilbao for demolition by D. Martin, Bilbao.

BROADHURST (II) at Shoreham   *G. A. Osbon*

70. BROADHURST (II) (1948-1968)
ON. 182903. 1171g, 561n, 1525d. 225'0" × 34'6" × 14'7¼"
7-cyl. 2SCSA oil engine by British Polar Engines Ltd., Glasgow.
11.1948: Completed by Grangemouth Dockyard Co. Ltd., Grangemouth. *17.10.1968:* Arrived at Blyth for demolition by Hughes Bolckow Ltd.

HENFIELD   *World Ship Photo Library*

71. HENFIELD (1949-1969)
ON. 183147. 1098g, 521n, 1530d. 225'0" × 34'6" × 14'7¼"
6-cyl. 2SCSA oil engine by British Polar Engines Ltd., Glasgow.
12.1949: Completed by Grangemouth Dockyard Co. Ltd., Grangemouth. *1969:* Sold to Ch. Valsamakis- A. Alexatos, Greece and renamed DANAE III. *1971:* Sold to other Greek owners and renamed TSIMENTEFS. *1971:* Sold to Georgios Stavrou-Nikolaos Zoulias & Co., (D. A. Stavrou O. E. Shipping Enterprises, managers) Greece and renamed THANASSIS. *1977:* Owners became Georgios Stavrou & Evangelos Malkogiorgos (D. A. Stavrou O. E. Shipping Enterprises and from *1978* Stavrou Management Co., S.A., managers) Greece. Still in service.

HEYSHOTT   *World Ship Photo Library*

72. HEYSHOTT (1949-1970)
ON. 182949. 2918g, 1586n, 4350d. 328'6" × 44'6" × 19'10½"
T.3-cyl. by North Eastern Marine Engineering Co. (1938) Ltd., Sunderland.
2.1949: Completed by S. P. Austin & Son Ltd., Sunderland as COLVILLE for Coastwise Colliers Ltd. *1949:* Bought by Stephenson Clarke Ltd., and renamed HEYSHOTT. *10.4.1970:* Arrived at Blyth to be broken up by Hughes Bolckow Ltd.

PORTSMOUTH   *Skyfotos*

73. PORTSMOUTH (1950-1971)
ON. 183239. 1805g, 953n, 2540d. 268'8" × 38'4" × 17'4"
8-cyl. 2SCSA oil engine by George Clark (1938) Ltd., Sunderland.
5.1950: Completed by John Crown & Sons Ltd., Sunderland. *1971:* Sold to Lygia Shipping Co.
Ltd., Cyprus and renamed SANADREAS. *1973:* Sold to Yellow Pilot Nav. Co. Ltd., Cyprus. *1975:*
Sold to Heron Navigation Co. Ltd., Cyprus and renamed OURANIOTOXO. *1976:* Sold to Nebraska
Shipping Enterprises Corp., Greece. *1980:* Sold for demolition to Bristol Channel Ship Repairers
Ltd., who began work *27.10.1980* at Cardiff.

MINSTER (II) as built   *G. A. Osbon*

74. MINSTER (II) (1950-1971)
ON. 183249. 1950-1964: 3194g, 1739n, 4800d. 335'4" × 46'0" × 20'0¼"
1964-on: 3647g, 2198n, 5420d. 375'0" × 46'0" × 20'0½"
5-cyl. 2SCSA oil engine by J. G. Kincaid & Co. Ltd., Greenock.
6.1950: Completed by Burntisland Shipbuilding Co. Ltd., Burntisland. *1964:* Lengthened. *1971:*
Sold to Thenamaris Corporation S.A., Cyprus and renamed ELANDI. *1971:* Sold to Narkissus
Shipping Co. Ltd., Cyprus. *1973:* Sold to Ore Maritime Co. Ltd., Cyprus and renamed ORE STAR.
1975: Sold to John S. Latsis, Greece and renamed PETROLA L. *1976:* Sold to Athene Shipping
& Trading Corporation (John S. Latsis, manager) Greece and renamed PETROLA 50. *1978:*
Transferred to Panamanian registry. Still in service.

BEEDING (I)   *World Ship Photo Library*

75. BEEDING (I) (1950-1970)
ON. 184300. 1950-1965: 1142g, 572n, 1597d. 225'1" x 34'8" x 14'9½".
1965-on: 1277g, 692n, 1700d. 244'0" x 34'7" x 14'6¼".
6-cyl. 2SCSA oil engine by British Polar Engines Ltd., Glasgow.
11.1950: Completed by Goole Shipbuilding & Repairing Co. Ltd., Goole. *1965:* Lengthened.
1970: Sold to John Kelly Ltd., Belfast and renamed BALLYMORE. *1975:* Sold to Champion
Shipping Co. Ltd., Cyprus and renamed BALTICA. *1976:* Sold to Caliber Marine Co. Ltd., Cyprus.
17.1.1977: Abandoned by her crew in a position 43.15N, 08.05E after striking an unidentified
object during a voyage from Spezia to Barcelona and developing leaks and a heavy list. Taken in
tow the following day she was beached near Toulon, 19.1.1977. Refloated during *2.1977* she
arrived *16.3.1977* at Marseilles. *21.9.1977:* Arrived in tow at La Seyne for demolition by Otto
Lazar.

EMSWORTH   *C. Parsons/World Ship Photo Library*

76. EMSWORTH (1950-1971)
ON. 184347. 1784g, 929n, 2540d. 267'2" x 38'3" x 17'2"
8-cyl. 2SCSA oil engine by British Polar Engines Ltd., Glasgow.
12.1950: Completed by Burntisland Shipbuilding Co. Ltd., Burntisland. *1971:* Sold to Nautical
Shipping Co. Ltd., Cyprus and renamed ANDORA. *1973:* Sold to Green Pilot Navigation Co. Ltd.,
Cyprus. *1975:* Sold to Naviera Royal Corporation S.A., Panama. *20.4.1976:* Arrived at Dordrecht
for demolition by H. P. Heuvelman B.V., who began work in *6.1976.*

ARDINGLY *World Ship Photo Library*

77. ARDINGLY (1951-1971)
ON. 184351. 1473g, 707n, 1900d. 253'5" × 36'6" × 15'6¾"
7-cyl. 2SCSA oil engine by George Clark (1938) Ltd., Sunderland.
1.1951: Completed by S. P. Austin & Son Ltd., Sunderland. *1971:* Sold to John Kelly Ltd., Belfast and renamed BALLYROBERT. *1977:* Sold to Oreosa Navigation Co. Ltd., Cyprus and renamed LUCKY TRADER. Still in service.

78. GOSPORT (1952-1972)
ON. 184707. 1824g, 901n, 2395d. 262'0" × 38'9" × 17'0"
8-cyl. 2SCSA oil engine by George Clark (1938) Ltd., Sunderland.
10.1952: Completed by S. P. Austin & Son Ltd., Sunderland. *1972:* Sold to Sanastasia Ltd., (P.G.M. Agencies Ltd., managers) Cyprus and renamed SANASTASIA. *1973:* Managers became Zed Marine Enterprises Ltd., renamed MASSYS. *1974:* Sold to Blue Pilots Navigation Co. Ltd., Cyprus. *1975:* Sold to Overtania Shipping Co. Ltd., Cyprus. *7.12.1977:* Foundered off the coast of Guinea in a position 09.14N, 14.58W after an engine room explosion had been followed by fire. She was on passage from Bulgaria to Apapa/Lagos.

GOSPORT *World Ship Photo Library*

TOTLAND   *World Ship Photo Library*

79. TOTLAND (1952-1974)
ON. 184751. 1570g, 777n, 2008d. 240'10" × 37'9" × 16'1½"
8-cyl. 2SCSA oil engine by British Polar Engines Ltd., Glasgow.
12.1952: Completed by Grangemouth Dockyard Co. Ltd., Grangemouth. *1974:* Sold to Alscot Shipping Co., S.A., Panama and renamed ASTROLAND. *1975:* Sold to Kissamos Marine Co. Ltd., Cyprus and renamed IVY. *1976:* Sold to Prassa Shipping Corporation, Greece and renamed AGIOS FANOURIOS V. *1977:* Venta Shipping Corp., became managers. Still in service.

80. HAYLING (1953-1970)
ON. 185854. 1837g, 891n, 2395d. 262'0" × 38'9" × 17'0"
8-cyl. 2SCSA oil engine by George Clark (1938) Ltd., Sunderland.
2.1953: Completed by S. P. Austin & Son Ltd., Sunderland. *1970:* Sold to Probatina Shipping Co. Ltd., Cyprus and renamed SAGEORGE. *29.4.1972:* Went aground off Koufonisi Island, S.E. Crete in a position 34.56N, 26.09.30E during a voyage from Ashdod to Genoa with phosphates.

HAYLING   *G. A. Osbon*

BORDE (II)   *World Ship Photo Library*

81. BORDE (II) (1953-1968)
ON. 185921. 3401g, 1768n, 4550d. 344'0" × 46'2" × 20'0½"
T.3-cyl. by North Eastern Marine Engineering Co. (1938) Ltd., Sunderland.
7.1953: Completed by S. P. Austin & Son Ltd., Sunderland. *1968:* Sold to Balmoral Shipping Corporation, Liberia and renamed BALMORAL. *1971:* Sold to International Activity Shipping & Investment Co., S.A., Panama and renamed EILEEN. *1977:* Sold to Aryl Inc., Panama and renamed ARYL. *5.5.1978:* Sidermar S.p.A. began demolition at Trieste.

AMBERLEY   *World Ship Photo Library*

82. AMBERLEY (1953-1973)
ON. 185953. 1934g, 918n, 2405d. 262'3" × 38'9" × 17'3¼"
8-cyl. 2SCSA oil engine by British Polar Engines Ltd., Glasgow.
9.1953: Completed by Grangemouth Dockyard Co. Ltd., Grangemouth. *2.4.1973:* Foundered off the Wash in a position 53.03N, 00.58E after developing a list during heavy weather while on passage from Goole to Shoreham with coal. Her crew was rescued by helicopter.

LAMBTONIAN   *World Ship Photo Library*

83. LAMBTONIAN (1953-1960)
ON. 165824. 2818g, 1517n, 4090d. 321'11" × 44'6" × 19'4"
T.3-cyl. by North Eastern Marine Engineering Co. (1938) Ltd., Sunderland.
1.1942: Completed by S. P. Austin & Son Ltd., Sunderland as LAMBTONIAN for Tanfield S.S.
Co. Ltd., Newcastle. *1953:* Bought by Stephenson Clarke Ltd. *19.3.1960:* Arrived at Dunston on
Tyne to be broken up by Clayton & Davie Ltd., to whom she had been allocated by British Iron &
Steel Corporation (Salvage) Ltd.

LEA GRANGE   *World Ship Photo Library*

84. LEA GRANGE (1953-1959)
ON. 165776. 2993g, 1643n, 4390d. 328'0" × 45'4" × 19'8¾"
T.3-cyl. by North Eastern Marine Engineering Co. (1938) Ltd., Sunderland.
12.1939: Completed by S. P. Austin & Son Ltd., Sunderland as LEA GRANGE for Tanfield S.S.
Co. Ltd., Newcastle. *1953:* Bought by Stephenson Clarke Ltd. *1959:* Sold to Costicos Cia.
Naviera S.A., Lebanon and renamed COSTICOS. *9.6.1973:* Arrived in tow at Istanbul.
1.10.1973: Demolition commenced at Halic by Mehmet Zeki Verel.

33

STEYNING (I)   *Skyfotos*

85. STEYNING (I) (1955-1971)
ON. 186220. 1637g, 764n, 2045d. 242'0" × 38'5" × 15'9½"
8-cyl. 2SCSA oil engine by George Clark (Sunderland) Ltd., Sunderland.
4.1955: Completed by Austin & Pickersgill Ltd., Sunderland. *1971:* Sold to John Kelly Ltd.,
Belfast and renamed BALLYWALTER. *1979:* Sold to Oldham Brothers Ltd., Liverpool and
renamed SALLYWALTER. *1979:* Sold to Delta Marine Trading Co., Egypt and renamed ABEER
DELTA. Still in service.

86. PORTSLADE (IV) (1955-1977)
ON. 186319. 1955-1968: 1797g, 879n, 2325d. 242'0" × 40'5" × 17'1"
            1969-on: 1937g, 988n, 2643d. 262'0" × 40'2" × 17'1"
8-cyl. 2SCSA oil engine by George Clark & North Eastern Marine (Sunderland) Ltd., Sunderland.
10.1955: Completed by Austin & Pickersgill Ltd., Sunderland. *1968-1969:* Lengthened by
Humber Graving Dock & Engineering Co. Ltd., Immingham. *1977:* Sold to Sassa Cia. Nav. S.A.,
(Dionisios A. Stavrou O. E. Shipping Enterprises, from *1978* Stavrou Management Co.,
managers) and renamed SASSA. *1980:* Sold to Tanit Shipping Co., S.A. (John Skouras,
manager), Greece and renamed AGIA ANNA. Still in service.

PORTSLADE (IV) as built   *Skyfotos*

34

PORTSLADE (IV) after lengthening

Brownell Collection

87. ARUNDEL (1956-1972)
ON. 187486. 3422g, 1754n, 4600d. 344'0" × 46'5" × 20'0"
T.3-cyl. by George Clark & North Eastern Marine (Sunderland) Ltd., Sunderland.
11.1956: Completed by Austin & Pickersgill Ltd., Sunderland. *1972:* Sold to Gino Gardella, Italy
and renamed BRICK DODICESIMO. Still in service.

ARUNDEL

World Ship Photo Library

SHOREHAM (II) after lengthening   *World Ship Photo Library*

88. SHOREHAM (II) (1957-1979)
ON. 187533. 1957-1969: 1834g, 918n, 2350d. 242'0" × 40'6" × 17'0"
        1969-on: 1950g, 1027n, 2754d. 262'0" × 40'2" × 17'6¾"
8-cyl. 2SCSA oil engine by George Clark & North Eastern Marine (Sunderland) Ltd., Sunderland.
2.1957: Completed by Hall, Russell & Co. Ltd., Aberdeen. *1969:* Lengthened. *26.6.1979:*
Stranded in Mount's Bay, Cornwall during a voyage from Llanddulas to Ghent. *5.7.1979:*
Refloated by P. R. Eurosalve Ltd., to whom she was sold and by whom she was sold to Lynch &
Sons (Metals) Ltd. *7.9.1979:* Arrived at Strood for demolition.

STANSTED   *Brownell Collection*

89. STANSTED (1957-1972) Tanker
ON. 187632. 1034g, 371n, 1250d. 223'3" × 35'7" × 13'1¼"
7-cyl. 2SCSA oil engine by British Polar Engines Ltd., Glasgow.
— The Company's First Tanker —
9.1957: Completed by Richard Dunston Ltd., Hessle. *1972:* Sold to Dublin Shipping Ltd., Irish
Republic and renamed RATHMINES. *1976:* Sold to Eviaki Shipping S.A., Greece and renamed
MARK VI. *1979:* Avlis Shipping Ltd., became managers. Still in service.

90. CHAILEY (1957-1969) Tanker
ON. 187638. 2175g, 1036n, 2470d. 287'4" × 42'2" × 16'2½"
8-cyl. 2SCSA oil engine by British Polar Engines Ltd., Glasgow.
9.1957: Completed by Grangemouth Dockyard Co. Ltd., Grangemouth. *1969:* Sold to Societa
Imprese Marittime e Navigazione S.p.A., Italy and renamed FILICUDI. *1975:* Sold to Sarda
Bunkers S.p.A., Italy. Still in service.

LANCING (II) as built   *Brownell collection*

91. LANCING (II) (1958-1978)
ON. 187744. 1958-1969: 1638g, 763n, 2045d. 242'0" × 38'5" × 15'9½"
1969-on: 1765g, 936n, 2253d. 262'0" × 38'2" × 15'5¾"
8-cyl. 2SCSA oil engine by George Clark & North Eastern Marine (Sunderland) Ltd., Sunderland.
3.1958: Completed by Austin & Pickersgill Ltd., Sunderland. *1978:* Sold to Lisca Shipping Co.,
S.A., Panama and renamed LANDING. Still in service.

LANCING (II) after lengthening   *J. K. Byass*

37

PETWORTH (II)   *G. A. Osbon*

92. PETWORTH (II) (1958-1978) Tanker
ON. 187749. 1266g, 452n, 1150d. 233'7" × 35'6" × 13'3"
7-cyl. 2SCSA oil engine by British Polar Engines Ltd., Glasgow.
4.1958: Completed by Clelands (Successors) Ltd., Wallsend on Tyne. *1978:* Sold to Petromar
Navigation Co. Ltd., Greece and renamed EFTYHIA. *1979:* Sold to Petrolines Nav. Co. Ltd.,
Greece. *1980:* Sold to Kiama S.A., Panama and renamed BARBAROSSA. Still in service.

93. CLEVELAND (1958-1964)
ON. 300792. 8619g, 5009n, 12700d. 478'1" × 62'3" × 29'1"
5-cyl. 2SCSA oil engine by J. G. Kincaid & Co. Ltd., Greenock.
11.1958: Completed by William Gray & Co. Ltd., West Hartlepool. *1964:* Sold to Yick Fung
Shipping & Enterprises Co. Ltd., Hong Kong and renamed VENICE. *1972:* Transferred to Somali
Republic registry. *1976:* Transferred to Panamanian registry. *1980:* Sold to The People's
Republic of China.

FIRLE   *G. A. Osbon*

94. FIRLE (1958-1976) Tanker
ON. 300785. 948g, 431n, 1000d. 211'2" × 35'1" × 12'11¼"
4-cyl. 2SCSA oil engine by British Polar Engines Ltd., Glasgow.
12.1958: Completed by Henry Scarr Ltd., Hessle. *1976:* Sold to Maldives Shipping Ltd., Maldive Islands and renamed COVODORO. Still in service.

PULBOROUGH II   *World Ship Photo Library*

PULBOROUGH II (1959) — See PULBOROUGH No. 65, above.

FRISTON   *Brownell Collection*

95. FRISTON (1959-1975) Tanker
ON. 300859. 948g, 431n, 1000d. 211'2" × 35'1" × 12'11¼"
4-cyl. 2SCSA oil engine by British Polar Engines Ltd., Glasgow.
4.1959: Completed by Henry Scarr Ltd., Hessle. *1975:* Sold to Maldives Shipping Ltd., Maldive Islands and renamed MALDIVE ADVENTURE. *1977:* Sold to Oriental Commercial Establishment, Saudi Arabia and renamed ENAYATALLAH. Still in service.

39

COWDRAY   *World Ship Photo Library*

96. COWDRAY (1959-1976)
ON. 300932. 1748g, 809n, 2130d. 245'3" × 39'10" × 15'11¼"
8-cyl. 2SCSA oil engine by British Polar Engines Ltd., Glasgow.
6.1959: Completed by Grangemouth Dockyard Co. Ltd., Grangemouth. *1976:* Sold to John Kelly Ltd., Belfast and renamed BALLYCASTLE. Still in service.

PULBOROUGH (III)   *Brownell Collection*

97. PULBOROUGH (III) (1959-1964) Tanker
ON. 300994. 942g, 459n, 1250d. 216'7" × 31'6" × 14'2"
8-cyl. 4SCSA oil engine by Ma. K. Maschinenbau Kiel A.G., Kiel.
1956: Completed by Rolandwerft G.m.b.H., Bremen as GERTRUDE WIENER for Tankreederei de Vries & Co., K.G., Germany. *1959:* Bought by Stephenson Clarke Ltd., and renamed PULBOROUGH. *1964:* Sold to Ottavio Novella, Italy and renamed CAPONERO. *1975:* Transferred to Ciane-Anapo Cia. di Nav. e Bunkeraggi S.p.A., Italy. Still in service.

STORRINGTON   *J. K. Byass*

98. STORRINGTON (1959-1978)
ON. 301031. 3809g, 2075n, 5000d. 345'0" × 49'0" × 20'0¾"
5-cyl. 2SCSA oil engine by J. G. Kincaid & Co. Ltd., Greenock.
12.1959: Completed by Burntisland Shipbuilding Co. Ltd., Burntisland. *1978:* Sold to Astakos Shipping Co. Ltd., Cyprus and renamed MILOS II. *1980:* Zoulias Bros. & Co., became managers. Still in service.

BRAMBER   *World Ship Photo Library*

99. BRAMBER (1960-1968)
ON. 169259. 1968g, 938n, 2480d. 264'11" × 40'2" × 16'11½"
T.3-cyl. by North Eastern Marine Engineering Co. (1938) Ltd., Sunderland.
6.1954: Completed by S. P. Austin & Son Ltd., Sunderland as GREENBATT for Newbigin Steam Shipping Co. Ltd., (E. R. Newbigin Ltd., managers) Newcastle. *1960:* Bought by Stephenson Clarke Ltd., and renamed BRAMBER. *1968:* Sold to Maldives Shipping Co. Ltd., (Maldivian Nationals Trading Corp. (Ceylon) Ltd., managers) Maldive Islands and renamed MALDIVE SAILOR. *13.11.1974:* Arrived at Karachi en route for Gadani Beach where demolition began in *1.1975.*

100. HORSTED (II) (1960-1966)
ON. 180659. 2034g, 1092n, 2960d. 283'7" × 41'0" × 18'0½"
T.3-cyl. by North Eastern Marine Engineering Co. (1938) Ltd., Sunderland.
9.1945: Completed by S. P. Austin & Son Ltd., Sunderland as MOORWOOD for Wm. France, Fenwick & Co. Ltd., London. *1960:* Bought by Stephenson Clarke Ltd., and renamed HORSTED. *11.1966:* Sold to Metaalhandel en Sloopwerken H.P. Heuvelman, Krimpen a/d Yssel and after removal of engines, etc., resold to Boele & Oosterwijk for use as a sand barge on inland waterways.

HORSTED (II) *World Ship Photo Library*

101. MIDHURST (1960-   ) Tanker
ON. 302524. 1960-1970: 1328g, 606n, 1760d. 229'8" × 40'4" × 14"0¾"
1970-on: 1473g, 729n, 2233d. 260"0" × 40'4" × 14'6"
6-cyl. 2SCSA oil engine of 960bhp by British Polar Engines Ltd., Glasgow. Speed 10¼ knots.
11.1960: Completed by Blyth Dry Docks & Shipbuilding Co. Ltd., Blyth. *1970:* Lengthened. In
the present fleet.

MIDHURST *World Ship Photo Library*

102. FERNHURST (1961-   ) Tanker
ON. 302570. 1961-1971: 1328g, 606n, 1760d. 229'8" × 40'4" × 14'0¾"
1971-on: 1473g, 729n, 2268d. 260'0" × 40'4" × 14'6"
6-cyl. 2SCSA oil engine of 960bhp by British Polar Engines Ltd., Glasgow. Speed 10¼ knots.
2.1961: Completed by Blyth Dry Docks & Shipbuilding Co. Ltd., Blyth. *1971:* Lengthened. In the
present fleet.

FINDON *World Ship Photo Library*

103. FINDON (1961-1973)
ON. 186868. 3432g, 1733n, 4520d. 344'0" × 46'3" × 20'0"
3-cyl. 2SCSA oil engine by Wm. Doxford & Sons (Engineers) Ltd., Sunderland.
5.1957: Completed by Austin & Pickersgill Ltd., Sunderland as RONDO for Pelton S.S. Co. Ltd., Newcastle. *1961:* Bought by Stephenson Clarke Ltd., and renamed FINDON. *1973:* Sold to Andromyk Shipping Co. Ltd., Cyprus and renamed INDON. *1973:* Sold to San East Marine Corp., S.A., Panama and renamed SAN SHINE. *1977:* Sold to Triocean Shipping Co. Ltd., Panama and renamed TRIUMPH ACE. *27.9.1977:* Stranded in a position 25.18N, 121.32E near Keelung during her first voyage under this name from Kaohsiung to Keelung. Later broken up as she lay by Ming Shieh Steel Mill Inc.

GILSLAND   *World Ship Photo Library*

104. GILSLAND (1961-1968)
ON. 302806. 5222g, 2639n, 8727d. 450'0" × 56'8" × 24'10"
4-cyl. 2SCSA oil engine by Wm. Doxford & Sons (Engineers) Ltd., Sunderland.
10.1961: Completed by Burntisland Shipbuilding Co. Ltd., Burntisland. *1968:* Sold to Cia. Argentina de Transportes Maritimos A.R.L., Argentina and renamed MARDULCE. *1976:* Sold to Bangladesh Shipping Corporation, Bangladesh and renamed BANGLAR JOY. Still in service.

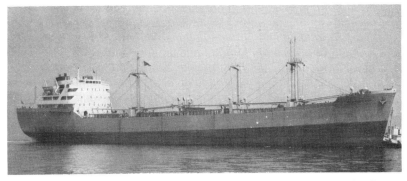

BLANCHLAND   *Alex Duncan*

105. BLANCHLAND (1961-1968)
ON. 302819. 8999g, 4987n, 12400d. 478'7" × 62'3" × 29'7"
4-cyl. 2SCSA oil engine by Wm. Doxford & Sons (Engineers) Ltd., Sunderland.
11.1961: Completed by William Gray & Co. Ltd., West Hartlepool. *1968:* Sold to Astro Acorde Cia Nav. S.A., Greece and renamed EUGENIA M. Still in service.

43

MAPLEHURST   *Brownell Collection*

106. MAPLEHURST (1961   ) Tanker
ON. 302839. 1961-1971: 1331g, 606n, 1760d. 229'8" × 40'4" × 14'0¾"
          1971-on: 1476g, 733n, 2282d. 260'0" × 40'4" × 14'6"
4-cyl. 2SCSA oil engine 1050bhp by Nydqvist & Holm A/B Trollhattan. Speed 10¼ knots.
12.1961: Completed by Blyth Dry Docks & Shipbuilding Co. Ltd., Blyth. *1971:* Lengthened. In
the present fleet.

107. DAVID MARLEY (1963-   ) Hopper Barge
ON. 304621. 730g, 337n, 1191d. 182'1" × 37'1" × 14'4¼"
4-cyl. 2SCSA oil engine of 980bhp by British Polar Engines Ltd., Glasgow. Speed 10 knots.
6.1963: Completed by R. Dunston (Hessle) Ltd., Hessle. In the present fleet.

108. ABBAS (II) (1963-1968) Liquefied Gas Carrier
ON. 182564. 943g, 512n, 668d. 207'5" × 31'3" × 12'4½"
6-cyl. 2SCSA oil engine by British Polar Engines Ltd., Glasgow.
6.1955: Completed by Scheepswerf "Gideon" v/n J. Koster Hzn, Groningen as the dry-cargo
vessel BROUGHTY (553g, 255n) for Dundee, Perth & London Shipping Co. Ltd., Dundee. *1962:*
Sold to Channel Shipping Ltd., Jersey. *1963:* Bought by Stephenson Clarke Ltd., and renamed
ABBAS. *1964:* Converted into a Liquefied Gas Carrier by Hawthorn Leslie (Shipbuilders) Ltd.,
Newcastle. *1968:* Sold to Cia. di Navigazione "Cossira" S.p.A., Italy and renamed CAPO CERVO.
1972: Transferred to Cryomar Cia. di Nav., Italy, and renamed CRYOMAR. Still in service.

109. FALSTONE (1964-   ) Hopper Barge/Sludge Carrier
ON. 305429. 359g, 182n, 502d. 131'0" × 26'10" × 11'9"
6-cyl. 4SCSA oil engine of 337bhp by Blackstone & Co. Ltd., Stamford fitted in 1964. Speed 8½
knots.
1934: Completed by L. Smit & Zoon N.V., Kinderdijk as the inland waterways hopper barge
AMSTERDAM VI for Dutch owners. *1964:* Bought by Stephenson Clarke Ltd., re-engined and
measured at 321g, 167n. *1966:* Converted into a Sludge Carrier of 359g. In the present fleet.

110. T.I.C. No. 18 (1965) Hopper Barge
ON. 145452. 592g, 237n, 174'7" × 32'1" × 12'8"
T.3-cyl. by the Shipbuilders.
7.1921: Completed by Fleming & Ferguson Ltd., Paisley as T.I.C. No. 18 for Tyne Improvement
Commissioners, Newcastle. *1964:* Sold to Thos. W. Ward Ltd. *1965:* Bought by Stephenson
Clarke Ltd. *1965:* Sold to Joseph Carney & Sons Ltd., Sunderland and renamed MILLSIDE.
5.10.1972: Arrived at Dunston on Tyne to be broken up by Clayton & Davie Ltd.

PULBOROUGH (IV)   *Alex Duncan*

111. PULBOROUGH (IV) (1965-   )
ON. 306515. 4995g, 2791n, 7665d. 369'11" (incl. B.B.) × 53'6" × 24'3"
9-cyl. 2SCSA oil engine of 2600bhp by British Polar Engines Ltd., Glasgow. Speed 12 knots.
4.1965: Completed by Blyth Dry Docks & Shipbuilding Co. Ltd., Blyth. In the present fleet.

112. SPRINGWOOD/ADDERSTONE (1965-   ) Hopper Barge
ON. 183252. 814g, 421n, 1106d. 185'6" × 36'1" × 13'9$\frac{1}{4}$"
5-cyl. 2SCSA oil engine of 820bhp by British Polar Engines Ltd., Glasgow. Speed 11$\frac{1}{4}$ knots.
6.1950: Completed by Lobnitz & Co. Ltd., Renfrew as SPRINGWOOD for British Electricity Authority (Stephenson Clarke Ltd., managers) London. *1955:* Transferred to Central Electricity Authority (same managers). *1.1.1958:* Transferred to Central Electricity Generating Board (same managers). *1965:* Bought by Stephenson Clarke Ltd. *1972:* Renamed ADDERSTONE. In the present fleet.

113. HORSHAM (1966-1972)
ON. 183074. 1759g, 1179n, 2735d. 270'6" × 39'6" × 17'1$\frac{3}{4}$"
8-cyl. 2SCSA oil engine by British Polar Engines Ltd., Glasgow.
8.1949: Completed by Hall, Russell & Co. Ltd., Aberdeen as MURDOCH for North Thames Gas Board (Stephenson Clarke, Ltd., managers) London. *1966:* Bought by Stephenson Clarke Ltd., and renamed HORSHAM. *1972:* Sold to Oslo Sand & Bergsalt A/S Norway for service as a storage vessel. *1973:* Renamed GRANITT. Still in service.

114. ROGATE (III) (1967-   )
ON. 309846. 4997g, 2861n, 7710d. 369'11" (incl. B.B.) × 53'6" × 24'3$\frac{1}{4}$"
5-cyl. 2SCSA oil engine of 3800bhp by Sulzer Bros. Ltd., Winterthur. Speed 12$\frac{1}{4}$ knots.
2.1967: Completed by Blyth Dry Docks & Shipbuilding Co. Ltd., Blyth. In the present fleet.

115. KEYNES (III) (1967-1975)
ON. 183256. 1771g, 1186n, 2730d. 270'6" × 39'7" × 17'0$\frac{1}{2}$"
8-cyl. 2SCSA oil engine by British Polar Engines Ltd., Glasgow.
6.1950: Completed by Grangemouth Dockyard Co. Ltd., Grangemouth as ACCUM for North Thames Gas Board (Stephenson Clarke Ltd., managers) London. *1967:* Bought by Stephenson Clarke Ltd., and renamed KEYNES. *1975:* Sold to Sigmami Cia. Nav. S.A., (Dionisios A. Stavrou O. E. Shipping Enterprises from *1978* Stavrou Management Co., S.A., managers) Greece and renamed TITIKA. Still in service.

116. CARGO FLEET No. 3/MEGSTONE (1967-1975) Hopper Barge
ON. 169150. 988g, 490n, 2230d. 207'2" × 35'0" × 15'0$\frac{1}{4}$"
T.3-cyl. of 650ihp by the Shipbuilders. Speed 8$\frac{1}{2}$ knots.
1.1946: Completed by Fleming & Ferguson Ltd., Paisley as CARGO FLEET No. 3 for Cargo Fleet Iron Co. Ltd., Middlesbrough. *1953:* Sold to South Durham Steel & Iron Co. Ltd., Stockton. *1967:* Bought by Stephenson Clarke Ltd. *1972:* Renamed MEGSTONE. *1975:* Sold to Belcon Shipping & Trading Co. Ltd.

ASHINGTON (I)   *J. K. Byass*

117. ASHINGTON (I)/ARLINGTON (1968-1980)
ON. 187534. 3894g, 2176n, 5630d. 356'7" × 50'6" × 21'9¾"
5-cyl. 2SCSA oil engine by Sulzer Bros. Ltd., Winterthur.
2.1957: Completed by Henry Robb Ltd., Leith as TENNYSON for Chine Shipping Co. Ltd.,
London. *1968:* Bought by Stephenson Clarke Shipping Ltd., and renamed ASHINGTON. *1978:*
Renamed ARLINGTON. *1980:* Sold to Gianna A. Shipping Co. Ltd. (Tirrenia Maritime Co. Ltd.,
managers) Greece and renamed GIANNA A. Still in service.

JEVINGTON   *J. K. Byass*

118. JEVINGTON (1968-1980)
ON. 300870. 5330g, 3269n, 7640d. 414'2" × 54'6" × 22'8½"
6-cyl. 2SCSA oil engine by Sulzer Bros. Ltd., Winterthur.
4.1959: Completed by Henry Robb Ltd., Leith as MACAULAY for Chine Shipping Co. Ltd.,
London. She was at that time a ship of 4655g, 2624n, 6670d with dimensions 366'11" ×
54'6" × 23'7". *1964:* Lengthened. *1968:* Bought by Stepehnson Clarke Shipping Ltd., and
renamed JEVINGTON. *1980:* Sold to Patmos Shipping Co. Ltd., Greece and renamed OMEGA
PATMOS. Still in service.

119. BIRLING (I) (1968-1975)
ON. 183166. 1771g, 1185n, 2730d. 270'6" × 39'7" × 17'0½"
8-cyl. 2SCSA oil engine by British Polar Engines Ltd., Glasgow.
1.1950: Completed by Grangemouth Dockyard Co. Ltd., Grangemouth as THOMAS HARDIE for
North Thames Gas Board (Stephenson Clarke Ltd., managers) London. *1968:* Bought by
Stephenson Clarke Shipping Ltd. and renamed BIRLING. *1975:* Sold to Puma Shipping Co. Ltd.,
(Medship Shipping Co. Ltd., managers) Cyprus and renamed EPIC. *1976:* Sold to Christincoast
Cia. Nav. S.A., (Dionisios A. Stavrou O. E. Shipping Enterprises from *1978* Stavrou Management
Co. S.A., managers) Greece and renamed CHRISTOFOROS. Still in service.

BOWCOMBE (II)   *World Ship Photo Library*

120. BOWCOMBE (II) (1969-1971)

ON. 186069. 3332g, 1678n, 4564d. 339'0" × 46'3" × 20'1¼"
T.3-cyl. by North Eastern Marine Engineering Co. (1938) Ltd., Sunderland.
5.1954: Completed by Hall, Russell & Co. Ltd., Aberdeen as SIR DAVID II for North Thames Gas Board (Stephenson Clarke Ltd., managers) London. *4.1969:* Bought by Stephenson Clarke Shipping Ltd., and renamed BOWCOMBE. *1971:* Sold to Gino Gardella, Italy and renamed BRICK UNDICESIMO. Still in service.

121. HARTING (I) (1969-1975)

ON. 185965. 1779g, 1175n, 2700d. 270'6" × 39'6" × 17'0¾"
8-cyl. 2SCSA oil engine by George Clark (1938) Ltd., Sunderland.
10.1953: Completed by S. P. Austin & Son Ltd., Sunderland as THOMAS LIVESEY for North Thames Gas Board (Stephenson Clarke Ltd., managers) London. *6.1969:* Bought by Stephenson Clarke Shipping Ltd. and renamed HARTING. *1975:* Sold to Knight Shipping Co. Ltd., (Medship Shipping Co. Ltd., managers) Cyprus and renamed COSMIC. *14.3.1976:* Arrived at Piraeus and laid up. *12.1978:* Demolition commenced at Piraeus by E. Pateraki O. E.

WILMINGTON   *Alex Duncan*

122. WILMINGTON (1969-)

ON. 337979. 5689g, 3264n, 8975d. 410'0" × 54'8" × 25'3½"
6-cyl. 2SCSA Burmeister & Wain type oil engine of 4200bhp by J. G. Kincaid & Co. Ltd., Greenock. Speed 13 knots.
9.1969: Completed by Hall, Russell & Co. Ltd., Aberdeen. In the present fleet.

123. FERRING (1969-)

ON. 338868. 1596g, 992n, 2833d. 285'0" × 43'2" × 17'4¾"
6-cyl. 4SCSA oil engine of 2520bhp by Mirrlees Blackstone Ltd., Stockport. Speed 12½ knots.
11.1969: Completed by Hall, Russell & Co. Ltd., Aberdeen. In the present fleet.

FERRING   *J. K. Byass*

124. BRIGHTLING (I) (1970-1971)
ON. 185872. 1762g, 1223n, 2675d. 270'6" × 39'7" × 17'0¾"
8-cyl. 2SCSA oil engine by George Clark (1938) Ltd., Sunderland.
3.1953: Completed by Grangemouth Dockyard Co. Ltd., Grangemouth as FALCONER BIRKS for North Thames Gas Board (Stephenson Clarke Ltd., managers) London. *1970:* Bought by Kyle Shipping Co. Ltd., (Stephenson Clarke Shipping Ltd., managers) and renamed BRIGHTLING. *1970:* Transferred to Stephenson Clarke Shipping Ltd. *1971:* Sold to Navale Cala di Volpe S.p.A., Italy and renamed CAPITAN ALBERTO. Deepened to 22'6" and her new data became 1843g, 911n, 3184d, 270'6" × 39'7" × 19'3". *1974:* Sold to Italsud Containers S.p.A., Italy and renamed FABIO SAVERIO. Still in service.

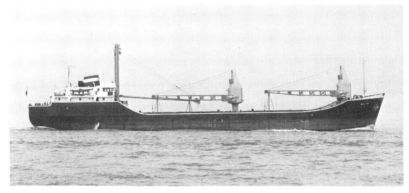

MALLING   *J. K. Byass*

125. MALLING (1970-   )
ON. 338953. 1596g, 992n, 2833d. 285'0" × 43'2" × 17'6"
6-cyl. 4SCSA oil engine of 2520bhp by Mirrlees Blackstone Ltd., Stockport. Speed 12½ knots.
2.1970: Completed by Hall, Russell & Co. Ltd., Aberdeen. In the present fleet.

126. CLIMPING (1970-1979)
ON. 187818. 1877g, 996n, 2835d. 275'2" × 39'5" × 17'1"
8-cyl. 2SCSA oil engine by British Polar Engines Ltd., Glasgow.
6.1958: Completed by Hall, Russell & Co. Ltd., Aberdeen as CAMBERWELL for South Eastern Gas Board. *4.1970:* Bought by Stephenson Clarke Shipping Ltd., and renamed CLIMPING. *1979:* Sold to Desguaces Heme S.A., who began demolition *3.1.1980* at Gijon.

TARRING   *World Ship Photo Library*

127. WORTHING (1970-1977)
ON. 187657. 1873g, 996n, 2835d. 275'2" × 39'5" × 17'1"
8-cyl. 2SCSA oil engine by British Polar Engines Ltd., Glasgow.
10.1957: Completed by Hall, Russell & Co. Ltd., Aberdeen as DULWICH for South Eastern Gas Board, London. *4.1970:* Bought by Stephenson Clarke Shipping Ltd., and renamed WORTHING. *1977:* Sold to Extro Marine Ltd., (Eurointerlink Ltd., managers) Cyprus and renamed WORTHY. *1980:* Sold to Antigone Maritime Co., S.A. Panama and renamed ANTIGONI P. Still in service.

128. TARRING (1970-   )
ON. 187771. 1877g, 996n, 2835d. 275'2" × 39'5" × 17'1"
8-cyl. 2SCSA oil engine of 1150bhp by British Polar Engines Ltd., Glasgow. Speed 10 knots.
4.1958: Completed by Hall, Russell & Co. Ltd., Aberdeen as LAMBETH for South Eastern Gas Board, London. *7.1970:* Bought by Stephenson Clarke Shipping Ltd., and renamed TARRING. In the present fleet.

WADHURST   *Brownell Collection*

129. WADHURST (1970-   ) Tanker
ON. 341042. 3819g, 2004n, 5470d. 374'11" × 48'11" × 21'5¼"
4-cyl. 2SCSA Burmeister & Wain type oil engine of 3180bhp by A/S Akers M/V Oslo. Speed 13¼ knots.
1962: Completed by A/S Stord Verft, Lervik as SAPHIR for Skips A/S Saphir (Edvin Endresen, manager) Norway. *10.1970:* Bought by Stephenson Clarke Shipping Ltd., and renamed WADHURST. In the present fleet.

BRIGHTLING (II)   *World Ship Photo Library*

130. BRIGHTLING (II) (1971-1973)
ON. 184709. 2002g, 1048n, 2760d. 271'6" × 39'4" × 17'6½"
8-cyl. 2SCSA oil engine by British Polar Engines Ltd., Glasgow.
9.1952: Completed by Burntisland Shipbuilding Co. Ltd., Burntisland as CORBRAE for Wm. Cory
& Son Ltd., London. *1969:* Transferred to Liquid Gas Tankers Ltd., (Cory Maritime Ltd.,
managers) London. *7.1971:* Bought by Stephenson Clarke Shipping Ltd., and renamed
BRIGHTLING. *1973:* Sold to Rio Vista Shipping Co. Ltd., Cyprus and renamed KAPPA JUNIOR.
1973: Zed Marine Enterprises Ltd., became managers and she was renamed ARBNAMA. *1973:*
Sold to Red Pilot Nav. Co. Ltd., (same managers) Cyprus and renamed VERZA. *27.3.1974:*
Wrecked two miles North of Roches Douvres Lighthouse, in a position 49.06.30N, 02.49W
during a voyage from Casablanca to Granville.

STEYNING (II)

J. K. Byass

131. STEYNING (II) (1971-   )
ON. 305432. 1594g, 979n, 2620d. 264'9" × 39'3" × 17'0¼"
6-cyl. 2SCSA oil engine of 1340bhp by British Polar Engines Ltd., Glasgow. Speed 11 knots.
1.1965: Completed by Clelands Shipbuilding Co. Ltd., Wallsend on Tyne as GLANTON for Sharp
Steamship Co. Ltd., Newcastle. *11.1971:* Bought by Stephenson Clarke Shipping Ltd., and
renamed STEYNING. In the present fleet.

BEEDING (II)

Alex Duncan

132. BEEDING (II) (1971-   )
ON. 342987. 1595g, 1114n, 3169d. 285'6" × 41'9" × 16' 3¼"
16-cyl. 2SCSA oil engine of 2000bhp by N. V. Appingedammer Bronsmotorenfabriek
Appingedam. Speed 12 knots.
12.1971: Completed by A/B Falkenbergs Varv., Falkenberg. In the present fleet.

ADDERSTONE (1972-) — See SPRINGWOOD, No. 112, above.
MEGSTONE (1972-) — See CARGO FLEET No. 3, No. 116 above.

ASHURST   *Michael Cassar*

133. ASHURST (1972-   ) Tanker
ON. 343124. 3451g, 2207n, 5360d. 366'5" × 51'2" × 20'0"
7-cyl. 4SCSA oil engine of 2700bhp by Maschinenfabrik Augsburg-Nurnberg A.G., Nurnberg.
Speed 12½ knots.
1964: Completed by Compania Euskalduna de Construccion y Reparacion de Buques S.A.,
Bilbao as the drycargo carrier FINSE (3651g, 2079n) for J. M. Johannesen's Rederi A/S Norway.
1972: Bought by Stephenson Clarke Shipping Ltd., renamed ASHURST and converted into a
tanker. In the present fleet.

134. ANGMERING (1973-1975)
ON. 307336. 1600g, 1045n, 2758d. 274'0" × 42'11" × 17'2½"
9-cyl. 2SCSA oil engine by British Polar Engines Ltd., Glasgow.
11.1965: Completed by Clelands Shipbuilding Co. Ltd., Wallsend on Tyne as RATTRAY HEAD for
A. F. Henry & MacGregor Ltd., Leith. *1972:* Re-registered in the ownership of Christian Salvesen
(Shipping) Ltd., Leith (who had taken over A. F. Henry & MacGregor Ltd., in 1964). *1973:* Bought
by Stephenson Clarke Shipping Ltd., and renamed ANGMERING. *29.1.1975:* Went aground on
Black Rock Shoal, Galway Bay while on passage from Gdansk to Galway with coal. Cargo
removed, but ship a Constructive Total Loss.

BRIGHTLING (III)   *J. K. Byass*

135. BRIGHTLING (III) (1975-1980)
ON. 363612. 1600g, 1088n, 3050d. 267'5" × 46'3" × 18'0½"
6-cyl. 4SCSA oil engine by Hijos de Barreras S.A., Vigo.
1972: Completed by Astilleros Construcciones, S.A., Vigo as BIRTE STEEN for Jorgen S. Steenberg Partrederi, Denmark. *1975:* Sold to Midland Montague Leasing Ltd., and Hambros Bank Ltd., London for service with Stephenson Clarke Ltd. *1978:* Stephenson Clarke Shipping Ltd. became owners. *1980:* Sold to Etty Shipping Enterprises Ltd., (Transmar Cargo Ships Inc., managers) Georgetown, Grand Cayman and renamed MOR STAR. Still in service.

DONNINGTON *Owners' photograph*

136. DONNINGTON (1975-)
ON. 365896. 7658g, 4839n, 11950d. 451'1½" (incl. B.B.) × 61'3¼" × 26'0½"
9-cyl. 4SCSA oil engine of 6500bhp by Stork-Werkspoor B.V., Amsterdam. Speed 14 knots.
8.1975: Completed by Verolme Scheepswerf Heusden B.V., Heusden. [Owners Midland Montague Leasing Ltd., and Hambros Bank Ltd]. *1978:* Registered in the ownership of M. H. Shipping Co. Ltd. (Stephenson Clarke Shipping Ltd., managers). In the present fleet.

137. DALLINGTON (1975-)
ON. 365968. 7658g, 4839n, 11950d. 451'1½" (incl. B.B.) × 61'3¼" × 26'0½"
9-cyl. 4SCSA oil engine of 6500bhp by Stork-Werkspoor B.V., Amsterdam. Speed 14 knots.
11.1975: Completed by Verolme Scheepswerf Heusden B.V., Heusden. [Owners Midland Montague Leasing Ltd., and Hambros Bank Ltd]. *1978:* Registered in the ownership of M. H. Shipping Co. Ltd., (Stephenson Clarke Shipping Ltd., managers). In the present fleet.

WITTERING *World Ship Photo Library*

138. WITTERING (1975-1976)
ON. 305758. 1599g, 1075n, 2650d. 281'6" × 41'9" × 16'9"
8-cyl. 4SCSA oil engine by Mirrlees National Ltd., Stockport.
9.1964: Completed by Goole Shipbuilding & Repairing Co. Ltd., Goole as FRAMPTONDYKE for Klondyke Shipping Co. Ltd., Hull. *1975:* Bought by Stephenson Clarke Shipping Ltd., and renamed WITTERING. *24.2.1976:* Collided 11¼ miles off Beachy Head with ODIN 999/75—m.v. during a voyage from Rotterdam to Cork with wheat. Abandoned, she capsized and sank *25.2.1976* in a position 50.43N, 00.37E.

139. FLETCHING (1976-1980)
ON. 187755. 1877g, 976n, 2835d. 275'2" × 39'5" × 17'1"
8-cyl. 2SCSA oil engine by British Polar Engines Ltd., Glasgow.
4.1958: Completed by A. Hall & Co. Ltd., Aberdeen as EWELL for South Eastern Gas Board, London. *1970:* Bought by Kyle Shipping Co. Ltd., (Stephenson Clarke Shipping Ltd., managers) and renamed FLETCHING. *1976:* Transferred to the ownership of Stephenson Clarke Shipping Ltd. *6.1980:* Sold to Eckhardt & Co. K.G., Hamburg and arrived *9.9.1980* at Gijon to be broken up by Desguaces Heme S.A., who began work *15.10.1980.*

WASHINGTON   *Owners' photograph*

140. WASHINGTON (1977-   )
ON. 377261. 6236g, 4078n, 8870d. 416'8½" × 61'3½" × 24'11"
12-cyl. 4SCSA Pielstick type oil engine of 6000bhp by Nippon Kokan K.K. Yokohama. Speed 14 knots.
5.1977: Completed by Kagoshima Dock & Iron Works Co. Ltd., Kagoshima. In the present fleet.

BIRLING (II)   *Owners' photograph*

141. BIRLING (II) (1977-   )
ON. 377461. 1584g, 1002n, 3860d. 299'5⅝" × 47'10" × 17'10⅞"
6-cyl. 4SCSA oil engine of 3300bhp by Mirrlees Blackstone Ltd., Stockport. Speed 14 knots.
12.1977: Completed by Clelands Shipbuilding Co. Ltd., Wallsend on Tyne. In the present fleet.

ALDRINGTON *Owners' photograph*

142. ALDRINGTON (1978-)
ON. 379697. 4334g, 2228n, 6570d. 339'11" × 52'9$\frac{1}{8}$" × 23'1$\frac{1}{4}$"
8-cyl. 4SCSA oil engine of 4800bhp by Mirrlees Blackstone Ltd., Stockport. Speed 14$\frac{3}{4}$ knots.
9.1978: Completed by Swan Hunter Shipbuilders Ltd., Wallsend. In the present fleet.

143. AMBER (1978)
ON. 185045. 1596g, 858n, 2410d. 267'9" × 39'0" × 17'0$\frac{1}{4}$"
8-cyl. 4SCSA oil engine by Klockner-Humboldt-Deutz A.G., Koln.
6.1956: Completed by Ailsa Shipbuilding Co. Ltd., Troon for William Robertson Shipowners Ltd.,
Glasgow, which company was acquired in *1970* by the Powell Duffryn Group and was in *1978*
integrated with the Stephenson Clarke fleet. *1978:* Sold to Simri Cia. de Nav., S.A., Panama and
renamed SIMRI. *24.12.1980:* Foundered off Cape Carbonara, Sardinia during a voyage from
Spezia to Benghazi.

AMETHYST *Skyfotos*

144. AMETHYST (1978-1980)
ON. 300208. 1548g, 856n, 2319d. 258'0" × 39'6" × 17'1$\frac{1}{4}$"
6-cyl. 4SCSA oil engine by Klockner-Humboldt-Deutz A.G., Koln.
7.1958: Completed by Ailsa Shipbuilding Co. Ltd., Troon for Gem Line Ltd., (William Robertson
Shipowners Ltd., managers) Glasgow which company was acquired in *1970* by the Powell
Duffryn Group and was in *1978* integrated with the Stephenson Clarke fleet. *1980:* Sold to
Surbuvan Shipping Co. S.A., (Sutas Shipping Services Ltd., managers) Panama and renamed
FAITH. Still in service.

ARLINGTON (1978-1980) — See ASHINGTON, No. 117 above.

BRILLIANT   *Brownell Collection*

145. BRILLIANT (1978)
ON. 300211. 1143g, 563n, 1442d. 224'3" × 33'9" × 14'6¼"
8-cyl. 4SCSA oil engine by Klockner-Humboldt-Deutz A.G., Koln.
10.1958: Completed by Scheepswerf "Gideon" v/h J. Koster Hzn, Groningen for Gem Line Ltd.,
(William Robertson Shipowners Ltd., managers) Glasgow which company was acquired in *1970*
by the Powell Duffryn Group and was in *1978* integrated with the Stephenson Clarke fleet.
1978: Sold to Inishmoyle Shipping Ltd., Panama and renamed SLEMISH. *1978:* Sold to
Shamrock Shipping (S) Pte. Ltd., (Shamrock Shipping Co. S.A., managers), Panama. *1979:* Sold
to Polybus Shipping Co., Panama. *1980:* Renamed BRILLIANTE. Still in service.

GEM   *J. K. Byass*

146. GEM (1978-   )
ON. 335059. 1599g, 1194n, 2920d. 304'2" × 43'9" × 17'0¼"
8-cyl. 4SCSA oil engine of 2150bhp by Klockner-Humboldt-Deutz A.G., Koln. Speed 12 knots.
10.1969: Completed by Nieuwe Noord Nederlandsche Scheepswerven N.V., Groningen for
Gem Line Ltd., (William Robertson Shipowners Ltd., managers) Glasgow which company was
acquired in *1970* by the Powell Duffryn Group and was in *1978* integrated with the Stephenson
Clarke fleet. In the present fleet.

147. JADE (1978-   )
ON. 361621. 1498g, 1173n, 2770d. 287'4" × 42'10" × 15'9¼"
8-cyl. 4SCSA oil engine of 1600bhp by Atlas-Mak Maschinenbau GmbH Kiel. Speed 12 knots.
Replaced in 1978 by an 8-cyl. 2SCSA oil engine of 1600bhp by the same manufacturers.
1967: Completed by Stocznia Gdanska, Gdansk as GDANSK (1200g, 850n, 2215d, with
dimensions 244'0" × 42'9" × 16'4") for Gerner Mathisen Rederi A/S Norway. *1970:*
Lengthened. *1973:* Sold to I/S Fondship (Erik Nuest, manager) Norway and renamed FONDAL.
1974: Bought by William Robertson Shipowners Ltd., Glasgow whose ships were in *1978*
integrated with the Stephenson Clarke fleet. In the present fleet.

148. PEARL (1978-   )
ON. 308579. 1598g, 1221n, 3130d. 301'10" × 43'11" × 17'1¼"
8-cyl. 4SCSA oil engine of 1800bhp by Mirrlees Ltd., Stockport. Speed 11½ knots.
5.1967: Completed by Goole Shipbuilding & Repairing Co. Ltd., Goole as SOMERSBYDYKE for
Klondyke Shipping Co. Ltd., Hull. *1978:* Bought by Stephenson Clarke Shipping Ltd., and
renamed PEARL. In the present fleet.

149. SAPPHIRE (1978-)
ON.307643. 1286g, 625n, 1660d. 227'10" × 36'7" × 15'6½"
8-cyl. 4SCSA oil engine of 1320bhp by Klockner-Humboldt-Deutz A.G., Koln. Speed 11 knots.
3.1966: Completed by Ailsa Shipbuilding Co. Ltd., Troon for Gem Line Ltd., (William Robertson Shipowners Ltd., managers) Glasgow which company was acquired in *1970* by the Powell Duffryn Group and was in *1978* integrated with the Stephenson Clarke fleet. In the present fleet.

TOPAZ   *J. K. Byass*

150. TOPAZ (1978-)
ON. 304135. 1597g, 835n, 2430d. 267'9" × 39'9" × 17'1¼"
8-cyl. 4SCSA oil engine of 2000bhp by Klockner-Humboldt-Deutz A.G., Koln. Speed 13 knots.
6.1962: Completed by Ailsa Shipbuilding Co. Ltd., Troon for Gem Line Ltd., (William Robertson Shipowners Ltd., managers) Glasgow which company was acquired in *1970* by the Powell Duffryn Group and was in *1978* integrated with the Stephenson Clarke fleet. In the present fleet.

TOURMALINE   *L. Schofield*

151. TOURMALINE (1978-)
ON. 304147. 1581g, 855n, 2430d. 267'9" × 39'9" × 17'1¼"
8-cyl. 4SCSA oil engine of 1800bhp by Klockner-Humboldt-Deutz A.G., Koln. Speed 13 knots.
11.1962: Completed by Ailsa Shipbuilding Co. Ltd., Troon for Gem Line Ltd., (William Robertson Shipowners Ltd., managers) Glasgow which company was acquired in *1970* by the Powell Duffryn Group and was in *1978* integrated with the Stephenson Clarke fleet. In the present fleet.

152. TURQUOISE (1978-1979)

ON. 301374. 1143g, 550n, 1643d. 228'0" × 35'10" × 15'0¾"
6-cyl. 4SCSA oil engine by Mirrlees, Bickerton & Day Ltd., Stockport.
3.1961: Completed by Clelands Shipbuilding Co. Ltd., Wallsend on Tyne as KYLEBANK for Kyle Shipping Co. Ltd., (Monroe Brothers, managers) Liverpool, *1970:* Management taken over by Stephenson Clarke Shipping Ltd. *1971:* Management transferred to William Robertson Shipowners Ltd., Glasgow. *1975:* Bought by William Robertson Shipowners Ltd., re-registered at Glasgow and renamed TURQUOISE. *1978:* Integrated in the Stephenson Clarke fleet. *1979:* Sold to Estland Maritime Inc., Panama and renamed ESTLAND. Still in service.

EMERALD   *Builders' photograph*

153. EMERALD (1978-)

ON. 377571. 1584g, 1002n, 3860d. 299'5⅝" × 47'10" × 17'11"
6-cyl. 4SCSA oil engine of 3300bhp by Mirrlees Blackstone Ltd., Stockport. Speed 14 knots.
4.1978: Completed by Clelands Shipbuilding Co. Ltd., Wallsend. In the present fleet.

ASHINGTON   *J. Appleton*

154. ASHINGTON (II) (1979-)

ON. 379883. 4334g, 2228n, 6570d. 339'11" × 52'9⅛" × 23'1¼"
8-cyl. 4SCSA oil engine of 4800bhp by Mirrlees Blackstone Ltd., Stockport. Speed 14 knots.
4.1979: Completed by Clelands Shipbuilding Co. Ltd., Wallsend. In the present fleet.

155. DURRINGTON (1981-)

ON. 390778. 7658g, 4839n, 11950d. 451'1½" (incl. B.B.) × 61'3¼" × 26'0½"
9-cyl. 4SCSA oil engine of 6500bhp by Stork-Werkspoor B.V., Amsterdam. Speed 14 knots.
15.1.1981: Completed by Verolme Scheepswerf Heusden B.V. In the present fleet.

156. HARTING (II) (1981-)

ON.   . 1584g, 1002n, 3860d. 299'5⅝" × 47'10" × 17'11"
6-cyl. 4SCSA oil engine of 3300bhp by Mirrlees Blackstone Ltd., Stockport. Speed 14 knots.
20.11.1980: Launched by Clelands Shipbuilding Co. Ltd., Wallsend for delivery Spring *1981.*

NORMANDY SHIPPING CO. LTD.

AUBE *World Ship Photo Library*

N.1. AUBE (1916-1917)
ON. 139145. 1837g, 1095n, 260.0 × 37.5 × 17.5 feet
T.3-cyl. by G. Clark Ltd., Sunderland.
8.1916: Completed by S. P. Austin & Son Ltd., Sunderland. *3.8.1917:* Torpedoed and sunk $3\frac{1}{2}$ miles N by W from Ile d' Yeu, South of St. Nazaire by UC.71.

N.2. SOMME (1916-1917)
ON. 139162. 1828g, 1091n, 260.0 × 37.5 × 17.5 feet
T.3-cyl. by North Eastern Marine Engineering Co. Ltd., Sunderland.
9.1916: Completed by S. P. Austin & Son Ltd., Sunderland. *24.2.1917:* Attacked by gunfire from a German submarine in the English Channel, but escaped. *30.3.1917:* Torpedoed and sunk 20 miles E by N from Cape Barfleur by UB.40.

SOMME *World Ship Photo Library*

N.3. TROSTAN (1918-1920)
ON. 87464. 1624g, 922n, 260.0 × 36.2 × 17.0 feet
C -2-cyl. by the Shipbuilders.
3.1883: Launched by Palmer's Shipbuilding & Iron Co. Ltd., Jarrow, Newcastle as JERSEY for "Jersey" S.S. Co. Ltd., (Morel Bros. & Co., managers) Cardiff. *1896:* Managers became Morel Ltd. *1911:* Sold to Shamrock Shipping Co. Ltd., Larne and renamed TROSTAN. *28.10.1918:* Bought by Normandy Shipping Co. Ltd. *1920:* Sold to The S. & R. Steamships Ltd., (Stone & Rolfe, managers), Llanelly. *1926:* Sold to J. N. Nilsson, Sweden and renamed UTKLIPPAN. *1932:* Owner became John S. Nilsson, Sweden. *1936:* Sold to J. T. I. Carlbom, Sweden. *1938:* Transferred to Torsten Carlbom, Sweden. *13.12.1942:* Sank off Gedsers Light Vessel, Island of Moen after collision with the German steamship OLDENBURG while on passage from Vesteras to Lubeck with iron ore.

N.4. MOYLE (1918-1923)
ON. 124668. 1761g, 749n, 275.2 × 36.1 × 18.6 feet
T.3-cyl. by the Shipbuilders.
11.1907: Completed by Ailsa Shipbuilding Co. Ltd., Troon as MOYLE for Shamrock Shipping Co. Ltd., Larne. *14.11.1918:* Bought by Normandy Shipping Co. Ltd. *1923:* Resold to Shamrock Shipping Co. Ltd. *21.5.1940:* Purchased by the Admiralty for use as a blockship and reported sunk *4.6.1940.*

N.5. BELTOY (1918-1923)
ON. 136351. 1544g, 732n, 250.7 × 36.2 × 17.2 feet
T.3-cyl. by the Shipbuilders.
7.1915: Completed by Ramage & Ferguson Ltd., Leith as BELTOY for Shamrock Shipping Co. Ltd., Larne. *13.12.1918:* Bought by Normandy Shipping Co. Ltd. *1923:* Resold to Shamrock Shipping Co. Ltd., (W. Lawson & A. R. Watson, managers). *1946:* Sold to Pace Bros., Malta (G. O. Till, manager, London). *1946:* Sold to Min Kiang S.S. Co. Ltd., China and renamed MIN CHIH. *1947:* Sold to Hai Ying S.S. Co. Ltd., China and renamed HAI NU. *1949:* Sold to Pacific Union S.S., Co., Panama and renamed AGUADULCE. Omitted from the *1955* edition of "Lloyds Register" owing to absence of recent information, but believed broken up in *1953.*

VAUX   *World Ship Photo Library*

N.6. GLYNN (1918-1923)
ON. 110509. 1106g, 450n, 230.3 × 33.1 × 16.0 feet
T.3-cyl. by Muir & Houston Ltd., Glasgow.
11.1899: Completed by Ailsa Shipbuilding Co., Troon as GLYNN for Shamrock Shipping Co. Ltd., Larne. *19.12.1918:* Bought by Normandy Shipping Co. Ltd. *1923:* Resold to Shamrock Shipping Co. Ltd. *1935:* Sold to Evangelos P. Nomikos (Petros M. Nomikos Ltd., managers) Greece and renamed AGHIOS NICOLAOS. *1941:* Taken over by the Ministry of War Transport, and placed under the management of Lambert Bros. Ltd. *1947:* Sold to I. Peltekis, Panama and renamed ROUL. *1951:* Sold to Orhan Sadikoglu ve Ortaklari, Turkey and renamed FEZA. *1955:* Sold to Haci Bekir Ali Muhiddin, Turkey and later in the year renamed TAYFUN. *1958:* Sold to Muhittin Topcu, Muzaffer, Tavioglu Yakup Uzuner, Turkey and renamed KERAMET. *9.1960:* Selamet ve Keramet Vapurlari Donatma Istiraki began demolition at Fener.

N.7. GRANSHA (1919-1923)
ON. 111364. 1192g, 487n, 235.5 × 33.1 × 16.6 feet
T.3-cyl. by Muir & Houston Ltd., Glasgow.
6.1901: Completed by Ailsa Shipbuilding Company, Troon as GRANSHA for Shamrock Shipping Co. Ltd., Larne. *20.3.1919:* Bought by Normandy Shipping Co. Ltd. *1923:* Resold to Shamrock Shipping Co. Ltd. *1934:* Sold to Soc. Eletherios Veliotis, Greece and renamed IOANNA. *1937:* Owners restyled as Eleftherios Veliotis. *21.4.1941:* Sunk by air attack at Patras.

N.8. VAUX (1920-1925)
ON. 144385. 1830g, 995n, 260.0 × 37.5 × 17.5 feet
T.3-cyl. by Richardsons, Westgarth & Co. Ltd., Sunderland.
3.1920: Completed by S. P. Austin & Son Ltd., Sunderland. *1925:* Sold to Fernand Bouet, France and renamed NANTAISE. *1928:* Owners became S. A. Armateurs Caennais (R. Bouet, manager) France. *1934:* Owners became Soc. Navale Caennaise (G. Lamy et Cie, managers) France. *1940:* Seized by German authorities following the occupation of France. *7.8.1943:* Torpedoed and sunk off Mudros by H.M. Submarine RORQUAL while on passage from Istanbul to Piraeus.

N.9. LYS (1920-1925)
ON. 144520. 1830g, 999n, 260.0 × 37.5 × 17.5 feet
T.3-cyl. by Richardsons, Westgarth & Co. Ltd., Sunderland.
5.1920: Completed by S. P. Austin & Son Ltd., Sunderland. *1925:* Sold to Westwick S.S. Co. Ltd., (J. Westoll, manager) Sunderland. *1929:* Manager became James Westoll Ltd. *1935:* Sold to Sovtorgflot, U.S.S.R. and renamed REFRIGERATOR No. 3. *1970:* Deleted from "Lloyds Register" owing to lack of recent information.

N.10. ANDELLE (1922-1925)
ON. 146229. 1832g, 992n, 260.0 × 37.5 × 17.5 feet
T.3-cyl. by Richardsons, Westgarth & Co. Ltd., Sunderland.
1.1922: Completed by S. P. Austin & Son Ltd., Sunderland. *1925:* Sold to Westwick S.S. Co. Ltd., (J. Westoll, manager) Sunderland. *1929:* Manager became James Westoll Ltd. *12.1.1940:* Requisitioned and *17.5.1940* purchased by the Admiralty for service as a Mine Destructor Vessel during which service she was extensively damaged *3.2.1942.* Subsequently repaired she was to have been converted at Swansea into a Minesweeper Maintenance Ship, but this work was not carried out and on *11.4.1945* she was handed over to T. W. Ward Ltd., who broke her up in *7.1945* at Briton Ferry.

NIVELLE *World Ship Photo Library*

N.11. NIVELLE (1923-1925)
ON. 147480. 1830g, 993n, 260.0 × 37.5 × 17.5 feet
T.3-cyl. by North Eastern Marine Engineering Co. Ltd., Sunderland.
5.1923: Completed by S. P. Austin & Son Ltd., Sunderland. *1925:* Sold to Fernand Bouet, France and renamed HONFLEURAISE. *1928:* Owners became S.A. Armateurs Caennais (R. Bouet, manager) France. *1934:* Owners became Soc. Navale Caennaise (G. Lamy et Cie, managers) France. *12.6.1940:* Sunk in the River Gironde by air attack.

MARIS EXPORT & TRADING CO. LTD.

ILSE   *Alex Duncan*

M.1. ILSE (1929-1942)
ON. 161337. 2844g, 1673n, 308.3 × 44.2 × 19.7 feet
T.3-cyl. by the Shipbuilders.
11.1929: Completed by Smith's Dock Co. Ltd., Middlesbrough for Maris Export & Trading Co.
Ltd. *1936:* Re-registered in the ownership of Stephenson Clarke & Associated Companies Ltd.
7.10.1942: Sunk by E-boat N.E of Cromer.

KYLE SHIPPING CO. LTD.

K1. KYLEBANK (1970-1971). See No. 152 in Stephenson Clarke list.

K2. BRIGHTLING (1970). See No. 124 in Stephenson Clarke list.

K3. FLETCHING (1970-1976). See No. 139 in Stephenson Clarke list.

FLETCHING   *J. K. Byass*

INDEX